Pretty
from the
Inside
Out

jennifer strickland

HARVEST HOUSE PUBLISHERS
EUGENE, OREGON

All Scripture quotations are taken from the Holy Bible, New International Version®, NIV®. Copyright © 1973, 1978, 1984, 2011 by Biblica, Inc.® Used by permission. All rights reserved worldwide.

Cover by Left Coast Design, Portland, Oregon

Cover photo © Shutterstock / Monkey Business Images

Backcover author photo by Natasha Brown Photography (www.natashabrownphoto.com)

Published in association with the literary agency of WordServe Literary Group, Ltd., www .wordserveliterary.com.

PRETTY FROM THE INSIDE OUT

Copyright © 2015 Jennifer Strickland Ministries, Inc.
Published by Harvest House Publishers
Eugene, Oregon 97402
www.harvesthousepublishers.com

Library of Congress Cataloging-in-Publication Data
    Strickland, Jennifer, author.
    Pretty from the inside out / Jennifer Strickland.
        pages cm
    Summary: "You're not a little girl anymore, and you'd love to start wearing makeup and pretty clothes, getting guys to notice you... But hang on a sec, girl! Before you get all made up, you need to make sure you know what it really means to be pretty. Pretty is... - the light you shine through your service - the way you show gentleness, humility, and respect - how you act when no one is watching. Jennifer Strickland used to be a model, and she knows that real prettiness comes from the heart. Join her on a journey of discovering true beauty--the beauty of a beloved daughter of God!"-- Provided by publisher.
    Audience: Ages 8-11.
    ISBN 978-0-7369-5634-5 (pbk.)
    ISBN 978-0-7369-5635-2 (eBook)
    1. Girls—Conduct of life—Juvenile literature. 2. Girls—Religious life—Juvenile literature. 3. Self-esteem in children—Religious aspects—Chrisitianity—Juvenile literature. 4. Self-perception—Juvenile literature. I. Title.
    BV4551.3.S78 2015
    248.8'2—dc23

                                                                            2014028186

Printed in the United States of America

15 16 17 18 19 20 21 22 23 / BP-JH / 10 9 8 7 6 5 4 3 2 1

For Olivia,
Our beloved daughter.
You are beautiful to me.

Acknowledgments

Even though lots of people poured love, hard work, and prayers into this book, I really just want to thank my husband, Shane, and our children, Olivia, Zach, and Samuel, for making it possible for me to be a wife and mom and at the same time an author and speaker. They have given up a lot of time with me so you can hold this book in your hands.

They've done this because they believe that aside from being a mother, I'm also meant to be a voice for Christ. On this page, I just want to thank them from the bottom of my heart for their love and sacrifice. Without knowing it, they have taught me the real meaning of beauty and opened my eyes to the wonder of the Father, who bestows upon us every good and perfect gift.

My sweet family is the good and perfect gift God gave me and continues to give me every day.

I hope this book blesses them in every way possible.

Contents

Introduction.................................... 7

1. The First Pretty Lie:
   You Are What Man Thinks of You........... 11

2. The First Big Beautiful Truth:
   You Are a Beloved Daughter................ 21

3. The Second Pretty Lie:
   You Are What You See in the Mirror......... 33

4. The Second Big Beautiful Truth:
   You Are a Precious Creation................. 43

5. The Third Pretty Lie:
   You Are What Magazines Tell You........... 53

6. The Third Big Beautiful Truth:
   You Are a Beautiful Temple................. 63

7. The Fourth Pretty Lie:
   You Are the Mask You Wear................. 73

8. The Fourth Big Beautiful Truth:
   You Are a Shining Light.................... 85

9. The Fifth Pretty Lie:
   You Are Mastered by the Media............. 99

10. The Fifth Big Beautiful Truth:
    You Are a Chosen Ambassador............. 113

Introduction

Who am I? As girls, that is the number-one question of our lives. Are you what people think about you? Are you what you see in the mirror? Are you the image in your pictures? Is your value decided by magazines, or even windows on a screen that disappear with a click?

Or are you worth *more*? Whether you are an actress, a singer, a dancer, an athlete, an artist, a cheerleader, or you aren't sure what you are good at yet, you are more than what meets the eye. You are more than what people think about you. More than the reflection in the mirror. More than what magazines say. You are God's beloved daughter, and he has great dreams for your life.

The problem with us girls is we have a tendency to measure our value by what we can see instead of by what we can't see. When a girl walks into a room, we start measuring her up. *How is she different from me? Is she better than me? Do people like her more?* we might ask. Or if it's a boy, *Does he notice me? Does he see me, the real me?*

As girls, sometimes we look in the mirror and see only the pimple on our face or the way our jeans don't fit or the stringy hair that we wish were curly or curly hair we wish we could tame. Maybe someone has pointed out our flaws or told us we weren't pretty—or told us we were—and we believed what they said about us. Maybe people have liked our pictures or criticized them, and we are starting to analyze them too. Or maybe we can't help but compare ourselves to the stars on TV and wish we looked like them or had all they seem to have. If you took a survey of every girl on earth, you would find out we have all battled with these things and fought to find our own identity.

This book is about that battle, and I want to help you win the war of who you are! We'll talk about five lies about your value, and then we'll learn to replace those pretty little lies with the big beautiful truths about who you *really* are and how valuable you are to God. These truths are like jewels in your crown that point to your true beauty, worth, and purpose.

We have a tendency to measure our value by what we can see instead of by what we can't see.

At the end of each chapter, you'll find messages from the Bible that will help you pave a beautiful pathway for your life with those precious jewels. **My goal is to help you see yourself in the reflection of God's mirror. Why? Because God's mirror is the only mirror that never changes.**

Before you get out of bed in the morning or go to sleep at night, take time to read a few of these pages so that you can be reminded of your worth from God's eyes.

Life is a journey. It doesn't start when you get through junior high, go to high school or college, or have a family of your own.

Your life begins now, and the choices you make today will determine the kind of life you have later!

No matter how busy you are, giving God the gift of your time is a gift you give to yourself. Ask him to pour truth into your heart—beautiful truth! As you go, when you discover little gems in the book that sparkle for you, mark them! You'll be able to look back later and see the valuable jewels God paved into your pathway when you were a girl.

I believe in you, I'm cheering for you, and I hope you see my love on every page.

Your friend,

Jen

Above all else, guard your heart,
for everything you do flows from it.
(Proverbs 4:23)

1

The First Pretty Lie:

You Are What Man Thinks of You

I used to think life started with the prince, but now I know I was a princess from the beginning.

A Man or a Mirror?

Have you ever wanted your daddy to be proud of you? Like if you could make his whole face light up, you would be the happiest girl? Or have you had a crush on a boy and found out he likes you too? That is the best feeling. When a boy thinks we are wonderful, we feel, well, wonderful.

But what if Daddy doesn't approve? What if Daddy doesn't show up at your performance? Or what if Daddy has problems of his own and can't seem to smile, even when you are twirling right in front of him? If you know what that's like, you know how crushing it can feel for Daddy not to love you the way you need.

Or what about when a boy says something mean about you behind your back or even to your face? Or a girl says, "So-and-so hates you." If you know what that feels like, you know how tiring it is to ride the roller coaster of people's opinions.

Our first "pretty little lie" goes like this: "If he thinks I'm pretty, I am pretty. If he likes me, I'm liked. If he loves me, I'm lovable." The flip side of this lie sounds like this: "If he doesn't want me, I'm not wanted. If she doesn't want to be my friend, I'm not popular."

This lie turns people into mirrors that reflect your worth. I was under the spell of this lie for a long time. Growing up, I had three best friends. No matter what I did right or wrong, they still loved me. But I also had some bullies in my life: girls who made fun of my flamingo legs, short, frizzy hair, and not-so-developed body. A few girls threatened to beat me up, and others just gave me cold, mean stares as I walked down the hallway at school. Boys, on the other hand, didn't even notice me until I was 15. So I grew up looking for their approval.

When I started modeling in elementary school, I saw that my daddy was proud of me. Once I got through junior high and my braces came off and my hair grew out, people in the modeling world started giving me approval for my pictures. We all want to have *something* we are good at…and it didn't feel like I was good at anything else.

But in the end, I found out that people make lousy mirrors. One day people liked me, and the next, they didn't. One day they said I was beautiful, and the next, they said I was ugly. One day they wanted to be my friend, and the next, they wanted someone else. So I believed this lie as much as I believed the sky was blue.

When we make people into mirrors, we end up on a roller coaster ride—because people change their minds about us. One year a girl says you're her best friend. The next year, she acts like she doesn't even know you. Or worse, she says mean things that really hurt.

Boys change their minds too. One day a boy likes a girl, the next day he doesn't know who he likes. In the fairy tales, as soon as the prince sees the princess, he never changes his mind about her—his love is forever! But that's not always how real life goes.

Fairy tales can help us understand why we grow up believing pretty lies. In fairy tales, before the princess meets the prince, she is just a common girl with no chance at happiness. But once the prince on the white horse shows up, everything changes. She is magically whisked away from the mother who belittled her, the stepsisters who were jealous of her, and the hard life she endured. The prince saves her and slays the enemy who tried to rob her of her place in the kingdom. When he asks her to marry him on bended knee, her true beauty and value are finally revealed. She transforms from a lowly girl dressed in rags to a beloved princess, gowned and crowned.

So the love of the prince changes her. His acceptance gives her worth. His protection determines a bright future. In fact, without him, she would have remained hopeless. So as little girls growing up with the fairy tales, we can easily believe that a boy gives us value. The truth is, however, you have value totally separate from the prince. The truth is, you were born priceless. No man can give you your value and no man can take it away!

In an ideal world, your parents would only show you how beloved and beautiful you are. In a perfect world, kids at school would treat you like you are precious. In the real world, however, people are not perfect.

If we always depend on other people to tell us how good

we are, we ride the roller coaster of approval. Some days, we get that approval; other days, we don't. If we focus our attention on comparing our looks, athletics, grades, or popularity, we can go all the way through school with no identity of our own. But **if we know *who we are*, we know that others don't define us. Others don't define your beauty. Others don't measure your worth.**

I learned this the hard way. For years, I was accepted and rejected based on how I looked. Sometimes I looked good. Other times, I didn't look good at all. When people praised me, I let their praise lift me up. When people put me down, I recorded their mean words in my mind and played them again and again.

When I was modeling, it was hard on my heart to have people criticize my appearance so much. Sometimes they would analyze the size and shape of my body, tone of my skin, and texture of my hair, and it made me feel like I was never good enough. I compared myself to the other girls, and that left me feeling insecure.

Maybe you know how that feels. Someone hurts your feelings and you let it sink in deep and weigh you down. Someone applauds you and you feel like you are walking on clouds. While these are natural responses, it's not healthy if we are relying on other people to make us feel good all the time. Our worth has to be something we decide on in advance—no matter how people treat us.

Big Beautiful Truth
You were born priceless. No man can give you your value and no man can take it away!

Our True Worth

Do you know your true worth? Do you know you are loved, precious, and beautiful? And no one gets to decide that you're not? If I had known my true worth growing up, I would not have let people's compliments or cruelty shape me so much. I would have decided that God's Word was the final word on who I was, since he was the one who shaped me from the start. And that's the truth that led me to leave the modeling industry and figure out what really made me happy.

The one thing I was good at in school was writing. I could work hard on a paper and get a good grade, and it didn't have anything to do with how I looked. But in modeling, if people critiqued my looks, there was only so much I could do about it. I became tired of feeling like I couldn't be the perfect mannequin they wanted me to be, and the pain built up inside. I became very depressed and turned everywhere for answers to the "who am I" question. Nothing worked, and I mean *nothing*. Until I began to pray for love.

Within weeks of those prayers, I met a girl in a small town in Italy who told me about Jesus Christ. She explained that God loved me and Jesus could heal my broken heart, and she promised to pray for me.

Shortly after meeting her, I met a group of people passing out Bibles in a park. They invited me to church and gave me my first Bible. I began to read it by candlelight, and in those pages, I discovered that Jesus loved hurting people. He loved the lost, the sick, the deformed, the confused, the rejected, and the misunderstood. He reached out to touch those our world doesn't want to touch, and he loved those our world doesn't love. And he didn't care if people approved of him or not. **He knew who he was, because he knew *whose* he was.**

Big Beautiful Truth
Our worth has to be something we decide on in advance—no matter how people treat us.

Jesus is the ultimate Prince. When we give our hearts to him, his love is forever. He is our heavenly Father, our Daddy, our safe place from the storm and the rain. He is the King of Kings, the One and Only. He gives you value above anything human beings can give to you. When he looks upon you, he stands up for you and smiles with the warmth of love.

When I gave my heart to Jesus and threw myself into his lap, I had been hurt deeply by people. I had also hurt myself trying to fill the emptiness in my heart. So when Jesus entered my life, I fell in love with a King who saw the princess in me even when on the outside I was a mess.

Jesus loves us despite the ways we fall short of perfect. He accepts us just as we are. He gives us value despite what people think about us. He is a Prince bent on rescuing us and a King who will come back for us on a white horse (Revelation 19:11).

It is a lie to believe that you are what people think of you. People's opinions can change. People, as good as they can be, will one day die. But the mirror of God never lies and never dies. He is forever, and his love for you is forever. When you give your heart to Jesus, you become his daughter—the daughter of a King. That makes you a princess forever and ever and evermore. And you should see his castle, his kingdom, the place he has made just for you!

God Is…

Jesus is the ultimate Prince. When we give our hearts to him, his love is forever. He is our heavenly Father, our Daddy, our safe place from the storm and the rain. He is the King of Kings, the One and Only.

Like a Breath

Jewel for Your Journey

Lord, what are human beings that you care for them, mere mortals that you think of them? They are like a breath; their days are like a fleeting shadow (Psalm 144:3-4).

When God created human beings, he made man and woman "in his own image." People are the only created beings made in the likeness of God. But people are *not* gods, so you must be careful to not let people define you. People don't decide your worth; God does.

Even though we are made in the image of God, people can die in an instant. Our jewel for today's journey says people are "like a breath" and our days are a "fleeting shadow." James 4:14 says man is "a mist that appears for a little while and then vanishes." Man is a "breath," a "shadow." Man is here one day and gone the next. His life is brief. People are not mirrors, and not gods.

We can love people, appreciate people, honor people, forgive, serve, and care for people—all of that is very important—but we cannot base our identity, value, or happiness on what people think about us. If we do, we are surely in for a roller coaster ride!

Remember, people are made in the image of God and deserve total respect and honor. But only God is a perfect reflection of you, and in the mirror of his face, every day, all day, you are valuable to him, no matter what people say about you. Don't hang your hat on people. Hang it on God, because he made you to be a reflection of him, and in the mirror of his face you are loved—always!

God Is Not a Man

Jewel for Your Journey

God is not human, that he should lie, not a human
being, that he should change his mind
(Numbers 23:19).

Have you ever noticed how often people change their minds? One day, a girl likes one boy, and a few weeks later, she likes another boy. Or maybe a friend changes her mind about you. People can be "shifting shadows."

The cool thing about God is that he doesn't do that. He says, "I am not a man!" "I do not lie!" "I do NOT change my mind." It's great to have someone in your life who will never lie to you, never change his mind about you. In fact, Hebrews 6:18 says it is *impossible* for God to lie.

Can you imagine having a relationship with someone who *can't* lie to you? Someone who is only capable of telling you the truth? That's having a relationship with God. His Word is Truth—and every day, it's up to you whether you are going to let people define you or God define you.

Here's another amazing thing about God: He won't ever leave you or turn his back on you. In life, there may be some people who turn their backs on you. That happens to *everyone*. Most of us deal with heartbreak, and we *all* deal with disappointment and death. People, as much as we love them, have the freedom to leave us or change their minds about us.

But God doesn't die, will never leave you, can't lie to you, and won't ever turn his back on you. That's pretty awesome. That's a solid foundation to stand on. So stand tall, princess. Hold your head high. God is on your side—forever!

Prince Charming or Prince Perfect?
Jewel for Your Journey
All have sinned and fall short of the glory of God
(Romans 3:23).

It is so easy to get confused with the *prince* thing. The fairy tales suggest the prince is perfect. He defeats the enemy; he rescues us; he makes our dreams come true.

If we believe a human prince gives the princess value, we may let boys decide for us if we are beautiful or ugly, worthwhile or not, and loved or unloved. That's a lot of power to give to a boy! In truth, not even a full-grown man has the power to decide whether we are wonderful or not! That's up to God!

Every human being falls short of perfect. The Bible warns us that no man can always say or do the right thing (James 3:2,8). But God makes no mistakes, and he will never use his words to hurt you. People, on the other hand, can make mistakes, especially with words. Sometimes people's words can be uplifting and helpful, and other times they can be destructive and hurtful—especially if they come out of the mouth of someone we love.

If people say mean things to you or about you, that doesn't mean they are right. Be careful not to let other people dictate your mood for the day. Don't give them the power to decide your value. Give that to God.

And remember, when you do meet a prince, he may be charming, but he'll never be perfect. Let God be the perfect one—the one true mirror that never changes.

A Prince or a Castle?

Jewel for Your Journey

It is better to take refuge in the LORD than to trust in humans. It is better to take refuge in the LORD than to trust in princes (Psalm 118:8-9).

Do you get your confidence from people liking you? Approving of you? Clapping for you? Or do you get your confidence from the Lord? It's easier to put our confidence in something we can see than to put it in God, whom we can't see. But it's something we *have to do* because only he can be our refuge.

A refuge is a strong fortress—kind of like a castle! So the princess runs to the castle to be safe from the storm. Princes can and should protect us, but only God is a castle that is never shaken. Those who put their hope in people will find themselves empty and dry, but those who put their hope in God will flourish like a healthy tree. Who will you make your refuge today?

2

The First Big Beautiful Truth:

You Are a Beloved Daughter

I put...a beautiful crown on your head.

EZEKIEL 16:12

My Prince, Mr. Charming

About four years after I invited Christ into my heart and left the modeling business, I met my prince, Shane. I realized it was him when we were riding horses on the beach!

We were on a road trip with my brother, traveling from San Diego to San Felipe, Mexico. When we arrived, the bright yellow sun was peeking over the horizon and I realized I had been smiling for hours. We set up camp, and Shane and I headed for a sunrise walk on the shore. We swapped stories and checked out seashells until the sun was radiant orange, beckoning us for breakfast. Shane cooked up sizzling bacon and eggs on the grill, and once we were done, without a wink of sleep, we headed for the sand dunes.

When he bartered for the four-wheelers and told me to hop on back, I admired how he took the lead without hesitation.

Dipping and diving on the massive hills of sand, we rode all day and then relaxed on the beach with a cold drink.

Trudging up and down the sand that blistering afternoon were tired, old horses with bored tourists on their backs. The horses were slow, and their saddles tattered and worn. As Shane and I watched this sad display, we leaned in and whispered, "I wonder if we could get those horses to run."

When it was our turn, we mounted and kicked, and like lightning, they bolted! The crowd on the beach saw those dirty horses coming at them in full gallop, and everyone ducked for cover. In San Felipe at midday, the tide goes almost a mile out, leaving sandy wet islands teaming with seashells and crabs. We took off for the islands. Water sprayed from the horses' hooves and the wind lifted us beneath its wings.

Riding on a speckled white stallion, Shane was thinking, *I'm a cowboy—there's no way this California girl is going to keep up with me!* But when he turned his head to see how far he'd left me in the dust, I was right there beside him.

I saw the sun flash golden light on his cheek. My heart skipped. *Oh my goodness,* I thought. *I've met my prince!*

I messaged my best friend when I got back. "I fell in love with a guy named Shane! We rode horses on the beach and I'm going to marry him!"

"Simmer down!" she wrote back. "We're not living in a movie!"

"Oh yes we are!" I responded. Shane and I saw each other every day after that. We were young and crazy in love.

Not long later, I strode down the aisle in a white gown woven with pearls and lace. I felt the warm kiss of the sun on my shoulders as I went down the runway to my groom, his eyes full of love.

When Shane and I took communion at the altar, I thought of the Cross. To have my prince wait for me, to treat me like I was *worth waiting for,* and to know God made me pure by the sacrifice of his Son—these are the most important truths of my life. I couldn't fight back the tears, even if they did mess up my wedding day makeup!

The Bible says, "Marriage should be honored by all" (Hebrews 13:4). Marriage is a picture of God's love for his church—Christ is the groom, and his people are the bride. Marriage is THAT special.

Keeping pure is something that starts for you today—not when you meet your prince. It's a mindset and a decision you make now that honors the most beautiful and powerful union on earth—that of husband and wife. You can begin honoring and praying for your husband now, long before you meet him!

Big Beautiful Truth
Keeping pure is something that starts for you today—not when you meet your prince.

God takes the hard things in our lives and transforms them into beautiful pictures. That's what he did for me on my wedding day. And that's what he can do for you *any* day.

Daddy's Girl

The desire for men to approve of us begins when we are little girls and we long for our daddies to tell us we are wonderful. It continues in elementary school and then junior high when we feel butterflies because a boy likes us. It goes on into high school and college when we feel more worthy because a boy wants to be with us.

Big Beautiful Truth
God takes the hard things in our lives and transforms them into beautiful pictures.

When I was a teen, I really didn't think that much about my modeling career. I thought about whether a boy paid attention to me or was going to ask me to the dance! Then when he ignored me or decided he liked someone else better, I felt bad and questioned my worth.

This natural longing for approval from men becomes unhealthy when we expect a boy or man—boyfriend, father, pastor, husband, teacher, coach—to be our answer to the questions, "Am I good enough? Do you see me? Am I wanted? Am I loved? And is there hope for me?"

The good news is that the answer to all these questions is YES. You are more than good enough. You are God's adored and cherished daughter—and you have a royal inheritance fit for a princess in store.

God works through many princely boys and men to instill our real beauty and value. Thank God for all the good men who believe you are precious and beautiful and worth waiting for…even worth dying for, as Christ showed you on the Cross.

When you can, it's best to surround yourself with positive voices who reinforce your true value. As much as possible, it is wise to stay far away from those who verbally, physically, or emotionally abuse you. If anyone treats you like you are less than valuable, that is about him or her, and not about you. Your value is engraved in the Word, and no one can take away what the Word of God says because it is forever (Isaiah 40:8).

The best thing the men in our lives can do is turn us toward God for our reflection. **We always see who we are in the mirror of who he is. Isaiah 64:8 says, "You, LORD, are our Father." In the reflection of that truth, we are his daughters.**

Fathers should be honored for the job they have, even if they're not perfect. Sadly, some fathers miss the mark of God's loving goodness. There are many fathers who don't know how to protect and guide their daughters. Some don't know how to be daddies. They don't know how to play with their little girls and help them grow. The troubles of their own lives might take over. Because of the pain they are in, some fathers search for a new life and leave their little girls behind. Some hurt you with their words. Some beat their little girls with their own hands. Many, many girls in the world are abused, and even more feel alone and afraid.

There is nothing more painful than hurts from a parent. It's very difficult not to let abandonment or cruelty sink deep into a little girl's heart and make her feel like she is not worthy, not loved, and not wanted.

Everybody wants to be "Daddy's girl" on earth, but not all of us are. Every single girl who gives her life to God, however, is "Daddy's girl" in heaven! Your identity as a beloved daughter of God isn't based on your relationship with your human father. It's based on your relationship with your heavenly Father.

The best thing girls can do is look up and ask our Father God to heal our hearts and show us what we look like in his eyes. And if we were blessed with a loving father and safe home, we bear a responsibility in loving the unloved girls of the world. There are girls walking down the hall at your school who feel alone and unloved.

What can we do for abused girls? We can pray for them. We can look for ways to reach out to them. We listen to their stories and show compassion. And we can show them the love of the Father.

There is a story in Ezekiel 16 about Israel, God's dearly loved people. The story pictures Israel as an abandoned baby girl. In the story, the baby girl is discarded like trash from the moment she is born. Naked and bare, she is kicking about in the rubble, bleeding and crying, completely defenseless.

But in this story, the baby girl is not truly alone, because God passes by and speaks to her. He says to her, "Live!"

That one word, *live*, helps her to blossom. Beneath the protection of the Father's love, she develops into "the most beautiful of jewels." She becomes a woman with long flowing hair.

God passes by this discarded daughter again, and this time he spreads the corner of his robe over her. He promises he will never leave her. She becomes his beloved bride, and God calls her "Mine." In tender compassion, he washes the blood off of her and anoints her with perfume. This is what Jesus does for us on the Cross—he takes our shame and washes us clean. Then he anoints us with the oil of his Holy Spirit and helps us stand tall again.

God puts leather sandals on the girl's feet, dresses her in a gown of expensive fabric, and drapes her with priceless jewelry. Finally, he places a beautiful crown on her head! "The splendor I [give] you [makes] your beauty perfect," he says to her (Ezekiel 16:14).

No matter where you've been or where you end up, God sees

you and says to you, "Live! Be mine! **The splendor I give you makes your beauty perfect!"**

If you are hurt, he sees it and he cares. If you are left alone, he is watching over you. If you are hurt, he can heal your wounds. If you are afraid, he will take care of you. And if you are hanging your head, he wants you to look up. When you do, he places a crown on your head.

The Crown
Jewel for Your Journey

My words come from an upright heart.
(Job 33:3)

I wonder what it would be like for you to remember every day that you wear a crown. Not a cheap plastic princess crown that could be worn for Halloween. No, a priceless crown, embedded with the world's most costly jewels.

It's a funny thing about a crown: You cannot slouch when you wear one. You cannot sink down in your seat and try to hide. You must stand straight and tall. If you were wearing a crown while walking down the hall at school, everyone would see it! And they would expect your behavior to match its majesty.

"Pretty" is more about behavior than about how you look. Real beauty is shown by the way you speak, act, dress, and treat people. It's about the choices you make. For example, it wouldn't sound pretty for bad language to spill from your lips while you are wearing a crown on your head. It wouldn't be pretty to roll your eyes at your parents or teachers! Or make rude comments and gossip about girls. It wouldn't look nice to hit your younger brother or scream at your mom while wearing a crown on your head, would it?

How would your life look different if every day you wore the crown of the Beloved daughter of the King? If your security didn't come from people, but from the King who calls you his?

A Buried Treasure

Jewel for Your Journey

The kingdom of heaven is like a merchant looking for fine pearls. When he found one of great value, he went away and sold everything he had and bought it (Matthew 13:45-46).

Did you know God sold everything he had to buy you? It's true! God had ONE Son, and he loved you so much that he gave him up in exchange for YOU.

The crazy thing is the world didn't recognize Jesus as God's Son. Some people did, but most did not. When he called God "Father," people called Jesus a liar. And when Jesus proved he was God's Son by miraculously healing a lame man, raising a little girl from the dead, and feeding thousands of people with a few broken loaves of bread, everyone did not bow down and call him King. Instead, they hung him on a wooden cross and made fun of him. God's one and only Son was literally bullied to death.

But what one man calls trash, God calls a treasure. Jesus has such great value that anyone who believes he is the Son of God has eternal life with the Father. He is so valuable that believing in him gives us a forever home in heaven. When you get there, the first person you will see is Jesus. And you will get to walk with him and talk with him all you want! There will be NO pain, NO wars, NO violence, and NO tears. Wanna go? Me too!

Jesus said, "I am the resurrection and the life. The one who believes in me will live, even though they die; and whoever lives by believing in me will never die" (John 11:25-26).

Do you believe this? If your answer is yes, then you can accept Christ as your Lord right where you are—*and* you can help a friend do it right where she is too!

Jesus told us that the kingdom of heaven is like a merchant looking for fine pearls. When he finds one of great value, he sells everything he has to buy it. The pearl he is talking about is you. You are a fine pearl of great value, and your heavenly Father loves you so much he sold everything he had to buy you.

How will you respond to that today? How will knowing you are a pearl change the way you live?

Secure in Love

Jewel for Your Journey

Let the beloved of the LORD rest secure in him, for he
shields him all day long, and the one the LORD loves
rests between his shoulders
(Deuteronomy 33:12).

I love reading this verse. When I think of it, I imagine myself crawling into my heavenly Daddy's lap and resting my head upon his heart, held by his strong arms. In that place, I am secure. I am safe. He guards me and all is well.

What thing in your life feels out of control? What scares you? What are you afraid of? Your Father wants you to come to him and allow him to be your shield.

Allow God to be your fortress, your resting place, and your security. Daughter, you are safe in his arms. You are the Beloved of the Lord, the "one the Lord loves," and you can rest between his shoulders. He will shield you all day long.

Hold on to Your Crown

Jewel for Your Journey

Hold on to what you have,
so that no one will take your crown.
(Revelation 3:11)

Every Disney princess had an enemy who was after her heart. Whether it was Maleficent hatching a plan to silence Sleeping Beauty, the Evil Queen trying to kill Snow White, or the Sea Witch robbing Ariel of her voice, there was always an enemy set on destroying the princess.

There is an enemy who wants to destroy you too.

The devil's goal is to separate you from God. If he can get you to question your parents and rebel against them, he will. If he can fill you with shame, anger, and fear, he will. If he can tie you up in jealousy and envy, he will. He is going to try to lead you into sin, which is disobeying God. He will make sin look delicious to you, like it will feel better than obeying God. He will attempt to get you to question God's and your parents' boundaries, telling you that you don't need them.

So what are you to do? First, you can pray in the name of Jesus. At the name of Jesus, the devil has to flee. Use your authority as the Daughter of the King to command the enemy to leave you alone and get out of your way.

No matter what the devil throws your way, make a decision

now to hold on to your crown. To wear it well, and to never, ever let anyone steal it from you. Your identity as a daughter of God is the only identity that is eternal. It is forever, and it gives you value that will stand the test of time.

Big girls fight with swords. We are not afraid of the devil and his schemes. We will not be shaken. We will stand tall, and we will fight the lies with the truth of God. We will fight, and we will win!

3

The Second Pretty Lie:

You Are What You See in the Mirror

*Magic mirror on the wall, who
is the fairest one of all?*

Magic Mirror on the Wall

What do you feel like when you look in the mirror? Do you smile at your reflection? Or do you wish you looked different?

Sometimes girls give the mirror too much power. They think, "If I look good, I am good; if I look bad, I am bad." That's a lot of power to give to a piece of glass that can be shattered with a hammer.

The second lie girls believe is "you are what you see in the mirror." The more we believe this lie, the more we can begin to feel like we aren't enough. We compare ourselves to women in swimsuit ads or to the most popular girls at school. Maybe we aren't skinny enough—or maybe we're too skinny. Our skin is not clear enough, our hair is not bouncy or straight enough, our eyes are not big enough. Our body is not the way we wished it would be.

Sometimes girls give the mirror too much power. They think, "If I look good, I am good; if I look bad, I am bad." That's a lot of power to give to a piece of glass that can be shattered with a hammer.

Some of us, on the other hand, admire our reflection, finding our value in our appearance. We might spend too long gazing. Instead of worshipping God, we begin to focus on and worship ourselves. Usually it begins as a desire to be pretty, to look nice, fit in, or take good care of ourselves. All of these are normal and healthy desires, but when we gaze over and over again at our own image, we can become so focused on our looks that we don't focus on others. This is not good. The mirror convinces us life is all about us and how pretty we look. But life is really about how we can bless others.

The world doesn't tell us this. Everywhere you go, you see pictures of perfect-looking women and girls. Those pictures can make us believe that the way we look matters more than the way we behave.

So we are tempted to focus on the outside, and it's easy to forget that *prettiness comes from the inside.* Beauty is a lot more about how we love people than how we look to people.

The mirror convinces us life is all about us and how pretty we look. But life is really about how we can bless others.

Always Changing

The reflection in the mirror will change your entire life. When you are growing from a tween to teen, your body will be changing you into a woman. It might feel strange or look funny to be going through so many changes, but it's a good time to notice that the mirror is always changing. You don't look the same now as you did when you were four, and you won't look the same when you are 14, 24, or 44.

When you become a teen, your body will grow in leaps, sometimes surprising you. Your body won't grow at the same pace as your friends', so don't focus on how they are growing or compare yourself to them. Stay in your own lane, realizing you have a race to run. It's your race, and you will do it at your own pace. Keep your eyes focused straight ahead, and don't focus on any other girls' race but your own.

I know what it is to be frustrated with the mirror. My tummy is soft no matter how many sit-ups I do; my hair is kinky and frizzy, as tough to tame as a lion's; and my skin gets pimples no matter how hard I beg it not to break out! I know what it's like to battle with the mirror.

Think of your mother. She doesn't look like she did when she was 16, you know! At one time, she may have had flawless skin and perfect hair. If she doesn't have that now, as most of us moms don't, does that give her any less value? **Is her beauty really measured by what you see or how she loves you?**

What about your grandmother? Do you think her body has changed in the last sixty years? Of course it has! Is her beauty measured by her reflection in the mirror or in the reflection of her face, in how she cares for you?

Big Beautiful Truth
Prettiness comes from the inside.
Beauty is a lot more about how we love
people than how we look to people.

Even when I was young in my modeling days, I had a tough relationship with the mirror. As a model, how I looked was ALL that mattered. From the time I was 8 years old to 22, looking pretty was my job. But when I was on the runway I kept trying to get skinnier. The less I ate, the worse I felt, and the worse I looked. I started getting dark circles under my eyes and my hair started falling out. I felt so ugly inside that I couldn't possibly look beautiful on the outside. I was treating my body like it was just a thing, not a creation of God, and that hurt showed up in my appearance. It always does.

Lots of girls believe the lie that I believed. Many, many girls at your school believe it. They have been called "fat" and "ugly," and to them, that translates as "worthless." A girl who thinks she is worthless treats her body that way.

On the other end of the spectrum, we also have girls who think they are valuable only because of how pretty they are. That is a lie too, and it can get them in all kinds of trouble.

We simply cannot base our value on something that always changes. If we do, we will always be on a roller coaster ride, confused about who we are and what we're really worth.

Never Satisfied

Are your friends all the perfect shape and size? Or are they different, a kaleidoscope of colors and shapes that each shine their own kind of light? Would it seem silly to you that your friends were unsatisfied with their reflections in the mirror? Probably, because you see their beauty in a unique way. But they may not. Almost every girl has a part of her body she doesn't like. Some girls even think, "I hate my body!"

When you don't feed your body properly, you can't think properly and you lose your joy for life. I lost that joy, and it took leaving modeling for me to find it again. I just had to learn to be me: the best me I could be.

We are more than what we see in the mirror. God cares so much more about the beauty of your heart and the way you show love to others than your messy hair or outfit.

The world tells us that if we are beautiful, we will be loved and happy. But this is a lie! Beauty comes from the inside. **Joy bubbles from someone who understands how to take care of her body in a healthy way. How to enjoy her body and appreciate it. How to enjoy food and exercise and sunlight and water. How to be the best she can be in the skin she is in.**

When Jesus died on the cross for you, he said, "You are worth it. You are beautiful. You are loved. You are mine. I made you in my image. I don't expect you to match the image *of* the world. I expect you to *be* my image *in* the world."

There is a God-sized hole in everyone's heart. No amount of food can fill it. Having the perfect clothes can't fill it. A number on a scale doesn't fill it. Being blonde or tan or athletic or fashionable doesn't fill it.

Only knowing you are God's beloved daughter and precious creation will fill it.

Big Beautiful Truth
We are more than what we see in the mirror.

A Fast from the Mirror

People think that because I was a model I never battled with the mirror. But that's not true. When I was in elementary school, my mother got me a haircut. When the hairdresser swung my chair around and I saw in the mirror how short my hair was, I started crying. But it got worse: She gave me a perm. A perm is when the hairdresser makes tight curls in your hair that don't come out for months—and the treatment smells horrible! After she added the curls, I was bawling. I hated it. I covered it by wearing a jacket with a hood to school for months.

To make life worse, I got big, thick, wraparound braces in third grade which made my teeth look like they were wrapped in tinfoil. To top it off, I broke both my elbows when I fell off the roof of our motor home and onto the concrete!

So I had tinsel teeth, bird's nest hair, and two broken elbows with huge casts and slings on both arms! Plus I was tall, which made me even dorkier.

In my teen years I started having acne. I battled it off and on while modeling. But it was when I was a grown woman, around the time I started teaching girls on "real beauty," that my skin had a horrible breakout. Pimples flared all over my forehead, cheekbones, and jaw. They were hard and red and grew in clusters on my chin. I cried when I looked in the mirror. I hated my skin. The more I focused on my skin, the worse it got.

We had just moved to a new town, and even though I wanted to meet new people, I didn't want anyone to see me like this. I tried treatments, creams, peels, everything. But none of it worked and the sores only got bigger and worse. My kids kept saying, "What is wrong with Mommy's face?"

At night when everyone was asleep, I would pound my fists on the floor, begging God to heal me. Out of desperation, I drove hours to meet a famous skin doctor.

But after examining my skin, he gave me one suggestion: Stop looking in the mirror.

"You are not an acne patient," he told me. "You are a heart patient. You have a belief in your heart that you have to be perfect. When your heart heals, your skin will heal." He told me to take a month off from looking in the mirror. "Focus on what makes you happy. Don't look in the mirror. Do what you love."

For forty days, I didn't look in the mirror. Instead, I spent that time reading the Bible and writing.

About three weeks into the fast I was dropping my son off at preschool and saw his teacher. "Jen!" she exclaimed. "You look radiant! What have you been doing?"

That morning, I had been reading the Bible. The Word says that it gives light to our eyes and radiance to our faces.

Something happened on my fast. I quit looking at myself and all my flaws and I focused on God. As I did that, I found out what I love and what makes me happy. I read the Word night and day, tromped the mountain trails, and counted stars. I laughed with my family and forgot what I looked like. I wrote my heart out. I finally told my story.

When my heart healed from the pretty lie that I "am" what I

see in the mirror, my skin healed too. I learned a lot about beauty during that fast. I learned that beauty is in the heart, and it spills out in our behavior. Beauty is more about the way we look at others than the way we look in the mirror. And I learned that when God looks at me, he calls me beautiful because I am his creation.

During my fast, I learned to see with my heart, and my heart got so much bigger for the people around me.

Beauty is in the heart, and it spills out in our behavior. Beauty is more about the way we look at others than the way we look in the mirror.

Breaking the Glass

I know what it's like to be young and to want to be perfect, and I know what it's like to realize perfect isn't possible. I know what it's like to look in the mirror and feel disappointed.

But I also know that the mirror is only glass. Someday it will disappear. I've decided I can't define myself by the way I look. When I turn away from the mirror I can look at the people I love.

Let's break the glass. Let's take a big ol' hammer and shatter the lies. Let's believe we are made for more than what we see. **Let's turn away from the slave of the mirror and shift our gaze to a mirror that never changes its mind about us.**

Is there really a mirror that never changes? A mirror that is satisfied? A mirror that reflects who we are and what we are worth?

Yes, there is.

The Fairest

Jewel for Your Journey

For we are God's handiwork,
created in Christ Jesus to do good works,
which God prepared in advance for us to do.
(Ephesians 2:10)

In *Snow White and the Seven Dwarves*, the evil queen is mesmerized with the mirror.

"Slave in the magic mirror, come from the farthest space!" she cries, the black wings of her cape arching behind her. "Through wind and darkness I summon thee: Speak!"

The mirror fills with flames.

"Let me see thy face!" she howls.

Through shadowy mists, a mask emerges. "What wouldst thou know, my queen?"

"Magic mirror on the wall, who is the fairest one of all?"

"Famed is thy beauty, majesty," the mask says. "But hold, a lovely maid I see. Rags cannot hide her gentle grace. Alas, she is more fair than thee...Lips red as a rose. Hair black as ebony. Skin white as snow."

"Snow White?" the queen rages, her ghoulish eyes swelling with fury.

We should pay attention to the way the mask in *Snow White* emerges from flames of fire—just like the devil dwells in the fiery furnace. Remember, princess, there is always an enemy trying to steal your destiny as a princess in the kingdom. If he can work through the mirror, he will. He will try to get you to focus so much on your appearance that you, like the queen, will play the comparison game with other girls. *Who is the prettiest?* you will ask, jealous of others' beauty.

The devil wants to trap you in jealousy, because when you are jealous, you are not celebrating the gifts in others and growing your own gifts. You are made to beautify the world. God put special treasures inside of you that make YOU unique. He made you to *do* good, not just look good. So don't be sucked in to the slave in the magic mirror. Instead, look at the One who made you, who created you beautiful to reflect him.

Being Renewed Day by Day

Jewel for Your Journey

Outwardly we are wasting away,
yet inwardly we are being renewed day by day
(2 Corinthians 4:16).

The Bible says your body is holy. So the way you care for your body and the way you see it matters. When we look in the mirror, we all want to be the best "me" we can be. That means we exercise, eat healthy, and care for our bodies. When it's time, we can also wear light makeup that highlights our features. We should dress our bodies beautifully in clothing that complements our figures—not too tight, too short, or too skimpy. We do not dress sloppily either, because we honor our bodies in a way that shows we are daughters of God. We present ourselves modestly with our own style and flair, reflecting the artistry of our Creator.

But while we do that, we remember that lasting beauty comes from the heart. We'll all grow old someday, and our bodies won't look young and strong anymore. But inwardly we can become more beautiful each day. No matter what our bodies go through, the Spirit of God within can glow brighter all the time. It's up to us to decide where our beauty truly comes from and ask God to fill us from the inside.

4 The Second Big Beautiful Truth:

You Are a Precious Creation

*I praise you because I am fearfully
and wonderfully made.*

PSALM 139:14

Barbie

Did you know that if Barbie were a real person, she would have to walk on all fours like an animal? Her feet and ankles are too tiny to support her weight. She wouldn't be able to lift her head up either—her neck is too thin!

But the sad thing is, girls all over the world think Barbie is a standard for beauty—even though she's not even real! Mattel, the toy company, gave them the Barbie doll as an image real girls could never match. Isn't that sad?

When I was a model, someone called my agency looking for a girl to play Barbie, and I got picked. I had to spend three hours in the hair and makeup chair to make me look like her! I was not happy, and I was so skinny I was sick. But no one knew that. When I was presented as Barbie, children ran toward me, all of them wanting to touch the bright pink silk of my gown.

Leaning down to greet them, I saw how they longed for me to look them in the eyes and smile. When I did, I knew they were fooled by the image of Barbie, thinking this doll was the picture of what it looks like to be pretty. But I knew then and I know even more now, beautiful isn't Barbie. Beautiful is the gleam of hope I see in children's eyes. Beautiful is you, right here, right now, with this book in your hands. Beauty is God in us.

Beauty isn't plastic. Beauty is God in us.

Eyes on God

When I first began reading the Bible, it felt like someone was feeding my empty belly with bits of bread dipped in sweet oil. **There is a spiritual food to the Bible that you can't find anywhere else. Its words are alive, and when you take in their beautiful truths, your heart gets fed.** The Bible did something magical for me. It began to fill my empty heart with living water. It turned my attention from how I looked to how Jesus saw me.

I didn't realize how focused on myself I had become. Like the queen in the magic mirror, I was fixed on my own reflection. Fixed on what was good for *me*, what was all about *me*, and how things affected *me*. But when we make ourselves the center of our worlds, we become dissatisfied, restless, and unhappy.

Christ was focused on others. We were "created in Christ Jesus to do good works, which God prepared in advance for us to do" (Ephesians 2:10). So when we root ourselves in Christ, we have a deeper purpose—God's purpose—and we bear good fruit, like joy, peace, patience, kindness, faith, hope, love. All of these things are the result of that one choice to live in Christ.

When we read the Bible, the focus gets off of us and onto a bigger God. A God who helps, heals, and holds us. When our eyes are on him, all things are possible. There is always more in God—more hope, more purpose, and more of a future.

Reading the Bible for the first time had such a big effect on me that I left a career I had pursued since I was eight years old! I wanted to find the bigger dreams God had for me. The Bible convinced me that walking with him was a greater adventure with a greater destination.

In the Kitchen

When I stopped modeling, I came home to what I had known as a child—my mother's cooking. On Sundays, Mom baked until the whole house filled with the scent of crisp brown chicken and juices steaming in the pan. She made thick, cheesy lasagna, gooey fudge brownies, carrot cake with cream cheese frosting, pumpkin bread, zucchini bread, banana bread galore. As a little girl I used to mix in the nuts, lick the bowl and spoon, and peek over the countertop at the steaming cakes.

These days I spend a lot of time in my husband's mother's kitchen. On any given holiday she will decorate the table like sweet Jesus is coming for dinner. Her Thanksgivings are filled with a brown-sugar-crusted sweet potato casserole, a tender brined turkey, rich giblet gravy, perfectly whipped mashed potatoes, and warm rolls with butter and jam. There is nothing so yummy as her famous chocolate pie, a recipe handed down from her grandmother, which my daughter will hand down to her children.

As we stand in Linda's kitchen, our hearts mingle like cups of flour, tablespoons of sugar, and pinches of salt. **As women and girls, we are knit together in the kitchen. Even in the most** difficult of times, there is power when women gather to cook a roast or bake a pie. It's as if the act of cooking is an act of faith, an act of love, an act of generosity. What we create in the kitchen are pictures of God's goodness working through us.

Getting back in the kitchen and cooking for the family again was a big part of my healing. Today, cooking for my husband and children is one of the most satisfying things I do. Food is a gift. Embrace it as a way to fuel your body and serve others. Eat in balance and enjoy your life. You only get one.

And if you ever feel like you are getting weird about food, ask for help. Pursue health and healing. Remember, our heavenly Father wants us to enjoy all the good things he created for us, including mashed potatoes, chocolate pie, and sweet whipped cream!

The Creator

In the Word, we see that God is our Creator. Creation is his specialty! He created the mountains and hills, the stars and the sea and everything in it. He created the entire amazing earth with all its fascinating animals. He created every tree, flower, fruit, and vegetable. He created man and woman in his image, and he was pleased with what he made.

We always see who we are in the reflection of who he is. He is the Creator, and we are his precious creations. He knit us together; we are fearfully and wonderfully made. Isaiah 64:8 says we are the clay and he is the potter; we are all the work of his hand. Like a potter forms a lump of clay on a potter's wheel to create a vase, God handcrafted you with incredible care. He formed your outward appearance and gave you gifts and talents. He even formed a space inside that only his spirit can fill, lighting you from the inside out.

Do you really think the makers of a plastic doll know more about beauty than a God who creates babies inside their mothers? Do you really think Hollywood knows more about beauty than our God who speckles the night with stars, sprinkles the hills with snow, and adorns the fields with wildflowers? Night and day, he splatters the world with his name: Creator. And he created you.

The Best We Can Be

As I see it, you have three options as a girl. You can obsess over your body, weight, and reflection, focusing on yourself all the time. You can make you and your body the primary focus of your time and attention, so that instead of worshipping God, you worship yourself. This option leads to a very unhappy life—so I wouldn't pick it!

The second option is that you can give up caring for your body, believing you will never be beautiful. You can treat your body like it's a trash can and fill it with junk. This option will lead you to become sloppy, overweight, and sick. This isn't a good plan either!

The third option is to accept the truth. "Outwardly we are wasting away, yet inwardly we are being renewed day by day" (2 Corinthians 4:16). Our bodies will change throughout our lives, and eventually they will "waste away." When our bodies die, we will return to our Creator in a renewed, spiritual body. In heaven, everything will be perfect.

But while we are here on earth, our bodies are the tents for our spirits, and we should care for them because they are valuable. Your body is precious because it was made by God. It will never be perfect and it will always be changing, but it is the house for your spirit. So exercise, eat right, and enjoy the body God created for his Spirit to live in.

Big Beautiful Truth
Your body is precious because it was
made by God.

We can each only be the best we can be in the skin we are in.
If I do that and you do that and our mothers and grandmothers and friends do that, we can leave this world imprinted with
real, lasting beauty—the kind that never fades away.

Grandma

We are going to close this chapter by thinking about our
grandmothers for a moment. Imagine your grandmother or
another older woman you know in a swimsuit. My goodness,
she looks old, doesn't she?

When I was a little girl, I used to go to my sweet Grandma
Betty's house and we would pick strawberries in her strawberry
patch and then take them inside and eat them with powdered
sugar. It was delicious, and I loved being with my Grandma Betty.

After my grandfather died, Grandma lived in a care center.
Like a tall candle long burned, her whole body dripped toward
the floor. But every time I would go visit her, she would look
through the peephole, swing open the door, and clap her hands
in delight. She was all lit up from the inside; her eyes sparkled
like jewels. Grandma just never got old in her spirit. All hunched
over but still bright and beautiful, she used to say to me, "You
know, I am the same person on the inside. I just look different."

The last time I held Grandma, I was about to give birth to
my daughter. Grandma was tired, so I lay on the bed with her
and rubbed the tense muscles around her tender spine until

she drifted to sleep. Two days later, I gave birth to Olivia just as Grandma was admitted to the hospital. But she never came home.

When I received the news of her death, I fell to the ground, weeping. I loved her so much, and all I wanted was for her to get to hold my baby girl, but she never got to.

Yet during those holy hours of caring for Olivia in the middle of the night, touching her soft baby skin, I felt the power of heaven's exchange. At one time Grandma held me; then, as she grew older, I held her. One day, when I am old, Olivia will hold me. **God always exchanges beauty for ashes, and it has nothing to do with what we see in the mirror.**

Someday, I will see Grandma Betty again, and she'll be standing tall and beautiful and young. She'll probably look up from her strawberry patch in heaven and clap her hands in delight when she sees me coming.

Not by Sight

Jewel for Your Journey

So we fix our eyes not on what is seen,
but on what is unseen, since what is seen is
temporary, but what is unseen is eternal
(2 Corinthians 4:18).

As God crafted the earth and everyone in it, he has filled you with depths of beauty that cannot be seen on the surface. It's your job to dive into the waters of your soul and discover the treasures there. It's up to you to carry those jewels to the surface and bless the world with your value.

What are you good at? What makes you happy? What love can you share? What gifts can you give? The answer to these questions can point you to God's plan for your life. When you do the "good work" he created you to do, you will feel fulfilled and happy.

Embrace the gorgeous truth: You are the precious creation of God. The weight of your worth is the weight of your heart; the palm of God, your only scale.

A Poor Reflection

Jewel for Your Journey

For now we see only a reflection as in a mirror;
then we shall see face to face.
1 Corinthians 13:12

When we look in the mirror, what we see looks like a perfect reflection. It looks crystal clear. But your reflection in the mirror is only a part of who you are. One day, you will see everything in its fullness. You will walk with God and talk with God in heaven's expanse. There will be no flaws. No accidents. No death. No sickness. Just joy.

What's cool about this is that even though we only see a "part" right now, God see it all. He wove us together before we were even born. He knows when we stand up and when we sit down. He knows what we're about to say before we even open our mouths! Everything about you, God already knows.

You are fully seen. And someday, you will see God fully too. So don't fix your eyes on what you see day to day. Fix your eyes on God—the perfect one who will come back for you and wash away all your imperfections.

The Artist
Jewel for Your Journey

God saw all that he had made, and it was very good
(Genesis 1:31).

God is a giver of gifts. The first thing he gave us was light. Then he created night. Next, he separated the waters by an expanse called sky. Then he made dry ground appear and called it *land*. Upon the land he created plants and trees. He gave us the stars, sun, and moon to be lights. He filled the water with living creatures and the sky with birds to fly across the expanse. He created livestock, wild animals, and creatures to move across the land.

Finally, he made man in his image to rule over the earth and the creatures in it. He gave the first humans plants, trees with fruit, and all the creatures in the whole earth for food.

He is a giver. A provider. A creator. And a master artist.

Not only is God your Father, but he is your Creator, "who made you and formed you" (Deuteronomy 32:6). Psalm 139:13 says he saw you even before you were born. He planned your days in the book of life before you lived a single moment. You are that important to him, that special.

Yet many girls believe they are not beautiful. Why? Because they do not get their image of themselves from their Creator. They get their image from the media. They compare themselves to young women they see online or on TV and think they are not enough.

But when you take in all that God created and realize that you too are "the work of his hand," marvelously made, you can change that. If you make your Creator your mirror, you will change the world around you by pointing other girls to God. And you, princess, will be a world-changer.

You are God's handiwork, his craftsmanship, his poetry (Ephesians 2:10). What will be the poem of your life that he writes through you?

5

The Third Pretty Lie:

You Are What Magazines Tell You

859 Ways to Get to Pretty

When we are little girls, our rooms tell a lot about us. Whether you decorate your room with twinkling lights, trophies, rock bands, dolls, bright colors, or horses, your room is a reflection of you.

When I was a girl, I collected dolls and masks. I loved their porcelain faces, mysterious eyes, and the silk fabrics they wore. As I got older, I replaced those dolls with posters of movie stars. In my teens, I created a big collage of pages torn out from magazines and pasted them on the back of my bedroom door. I loved the images of beauty, the stylish appeal, the stark poses.

I soon began appearing in magazines, and it was fun to see my picture on the printed page. Sometimes I liked the photos; sometimes I didn't at all! But it was the idea of being in them that was cool.

Over the years of modeling, I realized that image doesn't always match reality. **Perfect pictures don't mean girls are perfect.** Magazines paint women as flawless when in reality they are just as imperfect as the girls who read the magazines.

You know that feeling when you are standing in line at the

grocery store and the magazine covers are screaming at you to look at them? And then you see the girls in the pictures and quickly read the titles, and you get this icky feeling like it's all a lie? Or if it's all true, you aren't pretty enough? Or maybe you feel like you are supposed to look older than you really are?

Then you look up at your mom, and she is real. She doesn't match the magazine covers, and hopefully she tells you most of them are lies. Or maybe she peeks inside herself, looking for a new recipe or workout routine. But Mom doesn't match the image, and in a weird way, you are relieved. Because you know Mom is so much more than a picture on a page, and so are you.

I have a stack of magazine covers I've collected over the years. Let's go through some of the cover titles just for fun:

- 859 Ways to Look Pretty
- 656 Fashion and Beauty Ideas: Look Pretty Now!
- 624 Ways to Get the Most Out of Your Look
- 875 Ways to Look Beautiful
- 245 Winning Products for the Most Amazing Skin, Hair & Body
- How to Get Fresh, Clear Skin; Glossy Hair; Fast, Flattering Makeup; A Sleek, Smooth Body; and Bright, Flawless Nails
- Get Everything You Want This Year: Great Body, Tons of $$$, Amazing Clothes, and Mega Confidence!

According to the magazines, women have thousands of things they have to do, buy, and change about themselves to be pretty and fulfilled, when in truth, if you have Christ, you have everything you need for life.

You may be interested in style, design, makeup, and hair. That can be really fun for girls and there is nothing wrong with those things on their own. Most of us want good skin, cute outfits, fun shoes, and a new way to do our hair once in a while. At the appropriate age, that's okay! We are all called to be the best we can be in the skin we are in!

But there is also so much more to life than just looking pretty. **The world is not all about us and how we look. The world needs fewer girls focused on themselves and more girls looking outward.** There are people in the world who are giving their lives for good, and in my eyes they are the truly beautiful ones. Beauty is something that is so much deeper than how the magazines present it.

After only a few minutes of viewing a fashion magazine, seven out of ten girls begin feeling guilty, depressed, ashamed, and angry. Why? Because they are looking at unreal images of beauty that do not match their reflection in the mirror. What the world says is perfect is not real. It used to be publishers only airbrushed the *covers* of magazines. Now, *every single page* is computer generated, so *all* the images are fake—they are painted by an artist on a computer.

Instead of focusing on being the best we can be in the skin we are in, we can feel tempted to compare ourselves to those fake pictures.

Big Beautiful Truth
The world is not all about us and how we look. The world needs fewer girls focused on themselves and more girls looking outward.

The Bible says that people who compare themselves are not wise (2 Corinthians 10:12). When we compare ourselves, we lose track of the beauty and value we have as unique individuals handmade by God. And he never made us with the intention we would try to look, dress, and act like somebody else…especially the celebrities.

What is the effect of magazine images on girls? According to statistics, girls as young as six think they need to diet when they really don't! Over half of teens want to lose weight, and girls who are a healthy weight think they are fat. Little girls as young as ten are more scared of being fat than of our country being bombed!

If you feast on a steady diet of media images, you may become confused about what is truly important—like family, safety, and health. You might wallpaper your own mind with lies! So be careful what you focus your eyes on. Your eyes are the windows of your soul, and everything you see enters in.

The cool thing is it's up to *you* who you become. Despite what celebrities do or how they dress or flaunt their bodies, one of the greatest things you can do is respect yourself. If you respect yourself, you will not cheapen your body. You will dress appropriately, covering your body with cute clothes. When you honor your body, you honor your parents, God, and your future husband—and he's worth honoring even before you meet him!

Even when the real-life Disney pop stars turn down the wrong road, that doesn't mean *you* have to. You can choose to be a different kind of princess.

You will be a princess who remains a princess, who will never let anyone take her crown or her gown or her inheritance! Who you are as a daughter of the King and who you are as his precious creation will dictate how you treat your body. There is nothing more powerful than a princess who wears her crown well because she knows her value. She doesn't have to do 859 more things to be pretty; she just is pretty, because her heart belongs to God.

Big Beautiful Truth
When we compare ourselves, we lose track of the beauty and value we have as unique individuals hand-made by God.

The Messages of the Magazines

The world has one big lie that I want you to know about: "If something looks good, it is good." That's actually the first lie from the devil himself. The Bible tells us the devil was handsome to look at, but inside, he was wicked. He didn't want people to worship God; he wanted them to worship him. So war ensued in heaven, and the devil and a third of the angels were sent out forever.

The devil became a slithering snake who whispered in Eve's ear, convincing her to disobey God. He showed her that the tree was splendid to look at, and she fell for it. She ate from the one tree in the garden that God told her not to eat from. The result was disastrous. Her husband ate too, and they were sent out of the garden, separated from God.

God cursed the devil and told him he would always be eating the dust. Today, that devil is still up to his same old tricks—convincing God's children that if something looks good, it is good. But the truth is something may look pretty on the surface when it's actually ugly underneath.

The magazines make it look good to show off your body and to share it with others. You have to be wiser. You have to be able to separate truth from lies. The first big lie you see in magazines is that your body is not holy. The truth is, your body is connected to your heart and soul. God made your body holy and lives inside it. Your body actually belongs not to you, but to God. Your body has incredible value and should be treated that way!

The other lie you see in the magazines is *pretty* is all about how you look on the outside. In other words, it doesn't matter how you act. This is a terrible lie. I bet you know a girl who is pretty on the outside but not pretty in how she treats people. And I bet you would tell me she's not pretty at all! I also bet you know someone who is average-looking on the outside but who is delightful on the inside. That person makes others feel special, and I bet you think she is beautiful!

That is the way Jesus was. He was an average-looking guy who was not considered movie-star quality. In fact, he was a carpenter—a builder who worked with his hands. But crowds of people followed him everywhere he went. He is the most famous man in all the earth, and it isn't because of his great looks or amazing talent! It's because of his heart! People were drawn to the attractive qualities Jesus had within. They were drawn to the way he treated people, and that's what made him magnetic.

So let's replace those lies with truth. Your beauty comes from the love and respect you show others. It's compassion, service, humility, and hope. It's faith, joy, and never giving up. It's friendship, kindness, and truth spoken in gentle tones. Your beauty is not just what is seen on the outside; it is who you are within that makes you shine.

Your body is a temple—a holy place. You are so special. You are worth waiting for. You have value, and you have a voice. Use your voice for good. Use your voice for God. If you do, your voice will be a melody in his ears.

Big Beautiful Truth
Your beauty comes from the love and respect you show others. It's compassion, service, humility, and hope. It's faith, joy, and never giving up.

A Better Headline

What if we spent our time, money, and energy not only on *looking good* but also on *doing good?* What if you found a way to volunteer at the local preschool or homeless shelter or picked up the newspaper for the old lady down the street and dropped it on her doorstep for her?

What if you decided your value was more than your outfits, pictures, and pages, and it was about helping others?

What if the young women of this generation stood up and said, "I am MORE than my body! I have a heart and mind! My body is precious and I am worth protecting!" What if we all stood together and cried, "Beauty is not just what we look like; it is about how we love!"

It's time for women and girls to stand up and use their voices to speak truth. It's time for a better headline. Let's replace the lies of the magazines with the truth of our true value.

"Pretty Is as Pretty Does" could be the lead article of the magazine we could publish. We could give girls ten ways to encourage lonely kids at school. "I Am Loved," could be another article. We could show girls five ways to hold their heads high and keep their crown on even when life disappoints them.

I can see the titles of the articles I would publish: "Three Simple Things You Can Do to Stay Pure." "Ten Ways to Be the Best You Can Be." "Newsflash: Love Is Patient! Love Is Kind! Love Is Pretty!" Finally: "U R Holy! Beautiful! Precious! U R Made for More!"

A Fortress Around Your Heart
Jewel for Your Journey

Above all else, guard your heart,
for everything you do flows from it
(Proverbs 4:23).

This verse tells us that above all else, we are to keep a careful watch over our hearts. To guard your heart is to treat it as priceless. This verse doesn't suggest we take a casual watch over our hearts like we would a few cents. It says you must guard it as if it were your most precious possession.

In Rome you can visit a huge church called St. Peter's Basilica. Guards always stand out front. These men wear feathered hats and carry spears, but they also have bigger weapons to keep the area safe. They are there to make sure no one threatens the sacred church.

In your life, your parents are your guards. But the day will come when you have more freedom, and you have to be the guard over your heart. If you gaze too long at images that make you feel ugly, if you expose your mind to things you know are sin, or if you allow jealousy or hatred to take root in your heart, you aren't being a very good guard.

Everything you do in life will flow from your heart. Your friendships, family relationships, school, sports, performances—everything is an outpouring of your heart. So how can you be a vigilant guard over it? What do you need to protect yourself from? What will you allow inside the gates of your heart and what will you not allow in?

Perhaps you'll decide to not allow insults in. If someone insults you, the words won't get past the guards you've put in place! Maybe you'll decide you will only date when your parents feel it's time. Maybe you'll decide not to spend too much time on your iPad or iPhone if you have one because you don't want too many images wallpapering your brain. Maybe you'll protect your heart by praying every night that God would keep it pure and protect it. You may even want to take some time to write down some simple boundaries that will protect your most sacred treasure, your heart.

Test the Spirits
Jewel for Your Journey
Dear friends, do not believe every spirit,
but test the spirits to see whether they are from God
(1 John 4:1).

Kids see an average of 700 media images a day. That's a lot. Without us even realizing it, images can form our definitions for healthy relationships. We must remember that the media makes things look good that are really not good. The media tries to convince us that these things aren't sin, when in truth, they are.

Check out what the Bible says about this: "Woe to those who call evil good and good evil, who put darkness for light and light for darkness" (Isaiah 5:20). It's like he's saying, *How could you believe what is bad is good and what is good is bad? I'm against it, because it's going to cause you so much pain.*

First Thessalonians 5:21 says we are to test everything and "hold on to what is good." I want you to be able to test the spirits to see if they are from God. Don't believe everything you hear. Don't buy into the lie that if a picture looks good, it actually *is* good. You'll see pictures of girls wearing skimpy clothing and listen to songs about relationships God isn't pleased with.

Remember, the devil is a liar. He pretends to be an angel of light, but underneath it, there is danger in following his ways.

It might be an interesting adventure for you and your mom to take a trip to the bookstore and flip through some magazines. Together, see if YOU can practice separating truth from lies. I bet you'll be pretty good at it!

6

The Third Big Beautiful Truth:

You Are a Beautiful Temple

*How beautiful on the mountains are the feet of
those who bring good news, who proclaim peace,
who bring good tidings, who proclaim salvation.*

Isaiah 52:7

A Holy Place

You know those corner markets where you can buy chips and soda and gasoline? When I think of a convenience store, I think of a place where the floors are sticky with grime, the shelves are filled with junk food, and everything is cheap. Nothing is special. Nothing is valuable. Convenience stores aren't holy places; they are common places.

When people treat their bodies like convenience stores, they don't eat healthy or exercise. Maybe they even use drugs or allow people to touch their private parts. They don't understand that their bodies are sacred.

When you don't know that your body has value, you can end up with a lot of broken pieces in your heart that need to be put back together. You might feel rejected, alone, and sad.

In the Bible, Christ teaches us that our bodies are holy, and it matters to him how they are treated.

These three verses give a picture of how God sees your body:

> "Do you not know that your bodies are temples of the Holy Spirit, who is in you, whom you have received from God?" (1 Corinthians 6:19).

> "God's temple is sacred, and you together are that temple" (1 Corinthians 3:17).

> "The body...is...for the Lord, and the Lord for the body" (1 Corinthians 6:13).

When we accept Christ into our lives, he gives us his Spirit. His spirit is real. It is alive and it lives inside of us. It used to be that people went to the temple (or the church) to encounter God. Now, God encounters us. We are the temple. We are his dwelling place. Our bodies are his home. No matter what the world says, our bodies are not common places; they are holy places. We are temples of the Holy Spirit.

When I was a girl, I didn't really understand that my body was sacred ground. I don't think I ever really thought about it. I knew I was special, but I didn't believe deep down in my soul that I was a reflection of God, a daughter of God, and my body was his dwelling place. When you understand this, you put a higher value on yourself. When you understand who you are and whose you are, you protect your body in a different way.

You and I are holy ground. But when little girls are not treated like they are holy ground, they often grow up to become women who treat their bodies like they don't matter. Faith in Christ can wipe away any sin done in the body; faith in Christ makes us pure. But God wants you to know that your body should be protected. It should not be touched in private places. Your private places should be carefully guarded.

And if anyone ever hurts you by touching your body in the wrong way, you must—and I mean MUST—tell a trusted adult so you can get help. God knows if you are hurt. God sees it, and he will go to the ends of the earth, to the heart of the blackest night, to rescue his little girls from darkness. He wants you to know there is no end to his love for you. It is so far, so wide, so deep that nothing you ever do will be able to remove you from it.

No matter where you go, the Lord is only a cry away. The moment you cry for him, he will turn his ear to you and help you walk through the hardest moments of your life. He will use the pain to transform you into his beloved, cherished, and chosen daughter, who stands tall, strong, and free. You are cherished. You are worthy, and you are loved. Remember: Your body is God's house, and how you feel matters to him.

Holy Ground

When the Bible says your body is a temple of the Holy Spirit, what does that mean? What is a temple?

A temple is a place of worship, a sanctuary, a shrine; it is a place where you encounter God.

In the Old Testament, God delivered specific instructions for the building of his temple. He used precise measurements, just as he did when he crafted you. He used exact dimensions and decorated it beautifully, just as he did when he created you. On the inside of the temple, he told the people to inlay the floors with pure gold, just as he designed your heart to be pure. The interior walls of the temple were to be adorned with the most expensive jewels available—huge, priceless stones that reflect the elaborate worth of God's house. The temple was the most gorgeous place in all the world. It had no plastic. No junk. And no sticky floors! No one was allowed to enter into the temple without being holy in every way. They even had to take their shoes off to enter in because they stood upon sacred ground.

God creates us with the same kind of care. He paves the floor of your soul with pure gold and adorns the walls of your heart with priceless treasures.

That doesn't mean you are always going to *feel* beautiful or *feel* priceless, but it does mean you *are*.

Inside Out

If we do not guard our hearts carefully, the precious stones within us can become dirty and grimy. This can happen if we allow sin to live inside of us. Sin is anything that does not honor God. If we let jealousy, anger, fear, or pride live in the temples of us, these sins dirty the floor of our hearts and cover our gems with grime. The result? We don't shine. It is times like this when we must go to the Lord and ask him to clean us from the inside out.

Like most girls, I had things that hurt me. I locked those hurts up in my heart. I didn't know that I could take my hurts to Jesus and leave them in his hands. So instead, I let the pain and sadness build up inside me. When I sinned, I kept quiet about it because I didn't know I could confess to God and to my parents. I didn't understand that I needed to forgive the people who had hurt me. All of this was clouding my heart.

Maybe there is something in your life that hurt you. Someone who said unkind things. Someone who wasn't there for you when you needed him or her. Someone who makes you feel unimportant or dumb. Maybe you have told lies or have tried to keep things all for yourself and refused to share freely. Maybe you haven't forgiven someone or you have not obeyed your parents or been rude to your brothers or sisters. These sins will cloud your light. God hates all sin, and he doesn't want any of it to live in you.

Because we are the temple of God and he lives in us, he wants his house to stay clean. When we are honest about our sin, God forgives us by the grace of his son on the cross. But when we keep our sin hidden, we don't put it in God's light where he can turn it into something good. And that's his specialty—turning the yucky stuff into a beautiful gift. When we let him wash our hearts, we shine so much brighter. **When we allow him to be in charge of the temple of us, we are a pleasing home for him to live in.**

Your Beauty

Jewel for Your Journey

Let the king be enthralled by your beauty;
honor him, for he is your lord
(Psalm 45:11).

In the Bible you'll find many wonderful beauty tips, but they all have to do with your heart. Most of them pertain to the words you use and the way you treat people. First Peter 3:3-5 says your beauty comes from the inner self, your gentle and quiet spirit. That is Christ's spirit in you.

Now, you don't have to be a quiet personality to be beautiful to him. You can be expressive! The women who came falling at Jesus's feet in the Gospels were passionate and unreserved. But he called them beautiful because their passion was a reflection of him. They were humble. They were real. They were honest and told the truth about how they felt. He didn't accept them because they pretended to have it all together, but because he loved them.

The media doesn't define beauty as respect, gentleness, wisdom, and faith. But that is exactly how God defines beauty.

The question for you is whether you will go the way of the world or the way of the Word. Will you honor Christ as your king? Will you trust God enough to commit your body to him? Will you choose to honor your future prince now? Will your lips bring praise or cursing? Will your dress reflect God or the world? Who will you be? Which way will you choose?

When you honor the king with your body, mind, heart, and soul, he looks upon you and is enthralled with his princess bride. Your beauty has won his heart, and that lasts forever.

Forgiveness

Jewel for Your Journey

If you forgive other people when they sin against you,
your heavenly Father will also forgive you.
But if you do not forgive others their sins,
your Father will not forgive your sins
(Matthew 6:14-15).

Because I buried so many hurts in my heart, I ended up feeling sorry for myself. I felt like I didn't get a fair deal in life. Sin hurts, and the hurt creates a buildup of grime, kind of like a sticky floor.

I went through a time in my life when God had me take a close look at the temple of me. He helped me see I was angry at people who had disappointed me. Once his forgiveness washed me clean, he helped me forgive other people in return. If you feel angry or hurt about something, you may need to take a look at it. You may need to talk to someone about it, someone who can help you.

Forgiveness isn't always easy. You can't just sweep your hand across the sky and say, *I forgive everybody of everything!* You have to look each hurt in the face and say, "I forgive him or her for _____."

When we hold on to jealousy, resentment, or anger, we are just as caught up in sin as when we sin outwardly. God's heart for you is to be clean in every way. That's why confession and forgiveness are so important. When we refuse to confess our sins or won't forgive others, we stop up the flow of the Spirit in our lives. If we do not forgive, we will not be forgiven.

There was a time when I felt totally justified in my judgment of someone. I felt he had wronged me and I could not bring myself to forgive him. But one day I was called to court for a traffic ticket. As I waited for the judge, I thought about standing in front of God with the person I was mad at. I realized my sins were forgiven. God had given me a clean slate. Couldn't I give that to someone else?

So I forgave him. And when I approached the judge, he took my ticket and threw it away.

Because you have been given mercy, you are to be merciful. God forgives you; he has nothing but kindness, compassion, and grace for you. In return, you can show that same love to others. Forgiveness is not always easy, but it's a gift you give to your soul, and it keeps you free.

Maybe there is someone you need to forgive—a teacher who was harsh with you, a friend who turned her back, a father who left you, or a mother who hurt you in one way or another. Whoever it is, carry them to Jesus and lay them at the foot of the Cross. Their sins are too heavy for you to carry anyway. Jesus died for *all* sin. Let him take your burdens, your hurts, and your mistakes, and don't pick them back up again! Leave them at the Cross. Be who you are made to be—a Temple called Beautiful.

The Temple of You

Jewel for Your Journey

The glory of the LORD filled the temple.
(2 Chronicles 7:1)

It used to be that people purified themselves from sin by doing good things. But when Jesus died on the Cross, he made it possible for us to enter God's presence by believing in him.

When I first became a Christian, sin became uncomfortable for me. The Holy Spirit would whisper in my ear, *You know this is wrong* and lead me to repent from it—which means to stop it and choose never to do that again!

Believing in Jesus means you have forgiveness of all your sins—past, present, and future. But you still need to choose to live like you are a temple. Being pure is a choice.

When our daughter, Olivia, was ten years old, my husband gave her a purity ring that she wears on her ring finger. That finger will wear a wedding band one day. The ring she wears now is a symbol of an agreement between Olivia and her daddy. It means she will commit to be her "Daddy's girl" until the day she marries. It's an understanding that says her daddy will protect her and she will protect herself. When Daddy is there, he can watch over her. When he is not there, it is her responsibility to make sure she keeps guards at the gate—that she keeps her body pure by protecting it.

Other ways of choosing purity include staying far away from drugs, alcohol, and other temptations that cloud your mind and spirit. We also need to be careful what we see and hear on radio, TV, and the Internet. **In everything we do, purity takes self-control. It takes asking God to help you know when to walk away or turn away from something.** Ask him to tell you when to change the channel, shut down the computer, and choose an activity that brings blessing to your heart.

What kind of choices could you make that would help you to stay pure? How can you protect your heart, mind, and body? How would those choices affect your future? Ask God if there is a lifestyle choice you need to make to keep your purity.

7   The Fourth Pretty Lie:

You Are the Mask You Wear

Without our masks, we are accepted.

The Prettiest Girl in School

You are walking down the hall in school, and the prettiest girl you know walks by. She has all the right clothes, the right makeup, the right hair, the right friends. Everything about her seems right.

But the truth is, you don't know that about her. You have no idea what her life is like when no one's looking. Her home life might be much harder than we think. Her mom or dad might be having problems; she may have a brother, sister, parent, or friend who is sick or who has died or a best friend who has moved away. She may have secret heartache we know nothing about.

The truth is, no matter how someone looks on the outside—even if she has the perfect hair and her mom buys her the coolest clothes—you never know what's going on behind the scenes. And if you did, you might not sign up to be her, because I bet her life is not as perfect as you think it is.

Remember, when you've got your eyes on her, you've got your eyes off God. Comparing isn't wise. Stay in your own lane. You can't run her race anyway. You can only run yours. To get your attention back in the right place...

- Ask yourself what *you* have to be thankful for.

- **Remember who you are is not based on who she is.**

- Look beyond the surface to the heart. Just like your heart is the measure of your value, so is hers.

- Turn your eyes back to the mirror of God. He is your guiding light. He leads you in the paths that are best for you. Follow him.

The question for us will be whether we follow the popular girls in what they are doing or find our own path. When you follow God, you are bold. You are not afraid to forge your own journey. You find out what you are good at and pursue it, whether it's "cool" or not. Because the coolest thing on earth is to follow Jesus and to find his fantastic dreams for you. When you follow his lead, you will never go wrong.

Idol Fever

Recently, Olivia and I were watching *American Idol*, and she said of one of the judges, "She's perfect, Mom!"

I smiled. There's another one of our world's pretty big lies: "Perfect is possible." Yes, this idol judge looks gorgeous. Her makeup, skin, hair, and outfit are amazing! Even her laugh is contagious. *People* magazine called her "The Most Beautiful Woman in the World!"

But here's the truth: the same year that article came out and she was in TV commercials, music videos, and magazines looking so very pretty, she got divorced. Now her children live in two different homes.

If your family has experienced divorce, you know it's not pretty. It's painful. When love falls apart for movie stars, it hurts just as much as it does for us. We can't forget that just because things look good on the surface, that doesn't mean things are picture-perfect behind the scenes.

Yet the world we live in pays more attention to how things look on the outside than how things look on the inside. The world loves a pretty picture. But sometimes it's a masquerade— a dance where people wear masks and costumes and pretend to be people they're not.

I don't want you to think you ever have to put on a pretty smile and play the masquerade. You don't have to make yourself look good to cover hurt in your heart. You can be real about your hurt, you can get help when you need it, and you can trust your heavenly Father to bring beauty from ashes. He will do it. So when we see the pretty girl at school or on TV, we have to train our minds to rethink beauty. A beautiful girl is one who has a pure heart. In other words, her life behind the scenes, when no one is looking, is filled with God's love.

Is life all one big popularity contest? Is it about how many people "like" your pictures? Or is "pretty" more about the way we speak to our families at the beginning and end of the day, "perfect" more about the way we love the people in our lives, and "radiance" all about where we look for guidance? What if "beautiful" was defined by the time we spent on our knees in prayer when no one was looking? Or by how many people we helped that week?

Surely, we cannot just be as pretty as the pictures we see.

The Masquerade

As a kid I loved movie stars, rock stars, and other celebrities. They seemed glamorous and mysterious. But beneath the mask of success, many had broken hearts. Many of the biggest stars in our world have been terribly unhappy. They have to "wear a mask" to pretend that their lives are as amazing as everyone thinks.

I believe your gifts and talents are sacred. But some of today's stars don't see it that way. They don't see their gifts as responsibilities. But God does. With beauty and talent comes a responsibility to shine a guiding light that others will do well to follow. As girls, we have to discern what examples in Hollywood are worth following, and which are not.

Let's take Hannah Montana as an example. She was cute and sweet and everyone loved her. Costumes, T-shirts, backpacks, and posters with her image on it were everywhere we turned. Yet today, she has embarrassed herself and her fans in the way she dresses, the things she says, and the rude pictures she posts.

Most young stars fall. Most conform to Hollywood's image of celebrity life. Most drink and use drugs. Most don't wear their crowns well.

If we were so foolish as to follow the example of most young stars, we might believe that gowns, shoes, purses, makeup, hair, cars, and pocketbooks are more important than our behavior. As a girl looking at the images of the stars, you have to be able to separate truth from fiction.

- What defines you—your choices or the number of friends you have online?
- What counts more to God—your attitude or your popularity?

- What is life really about—how you look or how you
use your gifts to help others?

Only you can discover the answers to these questions for
yourself. God will help you. All you have to do is ask him and
listen for his answers.

Images of People

Many girls in your generation are in pain. Wherever I go, I
meet girls who are battling shame of some sort. They are bullied; they are abused; they are brokenhearted from their parents' divorces, their father's insults, or their mother's addictions.
They think they are ugly or fat or unlovable. They are obsessed
with their social media page (taking it down would be like cut-
ting off an arm!) and they are desperate for boys to like them.
The girls of this generation—not all, but many—are imitating
the behavior of the stars. But that doesn't make the girls happy.
When they get honest, they say it makes them sad.

The Bible has something very interesting to say about this. In
Romans 1:21-22, it says that when we worship *images of people*
instead of our Creator, our foolish hearts grow dark. The more
we fixate on *images of people* instead of on Christ, the more we
find ourselves feeling empty.

Some girls look for people's approval to make them feel better. Some scroll through thousands of images of girls on social
media and want to *look like her. Be like her. Be accepted like her.*
When this happens, girls struggle with feelings of jealousy.

It's easier to focus on what we *can* see than what we *can't* see.
You can see all those images passing across the screen, but you
can't see God face-to-face…at least, not yet. But 2 Corinthians

4:18 reminds us to "fix our eyes not on what is seen, but on what is unseen, since what is seen is temporary, but what is unseen is eternal."

In our world, we love to look at images of people. But the more we do, the more the devil's lies sink in: *I am not enough. I should do more. I should be more.*

Our foolish hearts become darkened, as the Bible says.

Deep down, every girl wants people to like her. Every girl wants people to say she is beautiful and gifted and has a great future ahead. And every girl wants someone to see beyond the mask she wears and love her for who she is on the inside. This is the longing of every girl, and it is never fulfilled through social media or people liking her pictures. Take it from a model who had thousands of "pretty pictures" in her life—wearing a mask of prettiness doesn't make anyone happy.

The thing that makes us happy is truth on the inside— beautiful truth: knowing that we are loved by Jesus and that in his eyes, we are enough. We are God's daughters, chosen by him to shine his light into the world. In his eyes, we are all stars.

Unmasked

The first girls' event I spoke at was called "Unmasked." When I arrived at the event, the girls were wearing matching bright blue shirts. They streamed into the building hugging their pillows and toting their overnight bags, huge smiles on their faces. They were probably excited that a former model was coming to speak to them. Or maybe they were happy just to get out of the house for a huge sleepover, which is the best part. I *love* sleepovers!

On Friday night, I shared my story. Then they went back to their host homes and poured out their stories to each other.

Big Beautiful Truth
We are God's daughters, chosen by him to shine his light into the world. In his eyes, we are all stars.

The next morning, something beautiful happened. As I spoke of my struggles with image and value, their struggles surfaced. They had issues with bullying, jealousy, purity, parents, weight, grades, and pressure of all kinds. You should have seen the relief on their faces as they talked about what was beneath *their* masks. Taking off their masks was the beginning of their freedom to be real and to know they were accepted. They didn't have to pretend to be perfect; they could be broken and loved. At times they laughed; at times they cried and came to support each other at the altar. On that day, they had the opportunity to trade in the lies they'd believed for the truth of who they were in God's eyes.

I fell in love with the girls—the skinny blondes, the tough athletes, the overweight beauties. I loved the misfits, the cheerleaders, the scholars, the dreamers. But my heart especially wrapped around the lonely and broken ones who didn't feel loved or precious—the ones who had believed they were *less* and needed someone to believe they were *more*.

Girls hide behind masks for several reasons. Sometimes they are afraid of getting hurt, so their mask is their wall, protecting them from a tough world. Sometimes their parents teach them to wear masks, making everything look good when it's not. Other times a mask is a way for a girl to look pretty on the outside when on the inside, she is hurting.

Deeper still, **masks hide our secrets. They are a way of**

pretending. But lies always surface, and no one feels good living a lie.

When I shed my masks and got real about what my life in the modeling industry was really like, it wasn't pretty at first. It was hard for my parents to hear, and it was hard for me to talk about. But over time, being honest about my fears and failures helped free me from them. I realized that if I had been telling the truth all along, I wouldn't have bottled up so much pain.

When we walk with Jesus, he always calls us to the truth. Yet it's up to us to make daily choices to walk in truth—to say that honesty on the inside is more important than how things look on the outside.

When we come to Jesus, there is no separation between us and him. He sees through our masks into our hearts. He calls us to truth because it is his language. He knows our truths and knows our lies. He knows our pain, and he knows how to heal it.

Being honest about what lies beneath the surface is a way to walk in the light. That means if you have a secret hurt burning in your heart that needs to be spoken, speak it to an adult you trust. When you put it in the light, that is Jesus's territory. You are safe in the light.

Getting Real

Sometimes you don't want to say out loud all the feelings you have in your heart. They're too overwhelming, and you don't know what to do with all your experiences. The fear of speaking builds a brick wall around you and traps you behind a mask. It's dark behind a mask, and hard to see. But if you stuff your very real emotions and hide your experiences for fear of being found out, you will get sick on the inside.

Keeping things locked up in the treasure chest of your heart does not allow sunlight to enter in, and things grow moldy in there! Instead, always let God and safe adults have the key to your heart. That way, they can help you air it out when you need to. The more sunlight you allow to shine on the jewels of your heart, the more they will sparkle.

In his life on earth, Jesus was most interested in people who took off their masks and were willing to say, "I need help." He called mask-wearers "whitewashed tombs," like people who tried to make a cemetery look pretty by painting it over.

God sees beyond the mask, and when you come to him, you can be real. If you have sinned, confess it. If you are angry, tell God. If you are hurt, be honest. He'd rather you cry out to him than pretend you don't need him to help you. When we open our hearts bare before God, his Spirit is with us, and we are free. Free to be a mess. Free to question. Free to be mad, to be honest, to be real.

When you approach God, you come into the light, and the more you encounter the light, the more you reflect it—like a jewel.

Holy

Jewel for Your Journey

Be holy because I, the LORD your God, am holy
(Leviticus 19:2).

We see who we are in the reflection of who God is. He is the Father; we are his daughters. He is the Creator; we are his creations. He is the Lord; we are the temples. He is holy; we are holy too. So it's important for us to understand what *holiness* means.

In Romans 12:1, Paul *urges* us to offer our bodies as "a living sacrifice, holy and pleasing to God." Does that mean you have to be perfect? No. But it does mean you need to see your body the way he sees it.

Ultimately, you are the one who decides: *My body is holy ground. I am the Temple of the Lord Jesus Christ, and I will not allow anyone to treat me as less than that.*

There is something so powerful about a girl who knows who she is. She attracts godly people because she has already decided to be godly. She is beautiful because she doesn't get her notions of beauty from the pattern of the world. She knows what the pretty lies are, and she believes the truth. She knows she is God's daughter, holy and set apart. And she knows she has a voice. She can ask for help when she needs it, and God will help her.

Make a decision today to be holy, and trust the Holy Spirit to help you.

Like the Sun

Jewel for Your Journey

There he was transfigured before them.
His face shone like the sun, and his clothes
became as white as the light
(Matthew 17:2).

Jesus had an inner circle of close friends. He didn't blab his deepest secrets to lots of people. First of all, his deepest secrets would be too overwhelming for everyone to know. Second, he knew the power of a tight-knit circle of trusted friends.

Jesus spoke to lots of people, teaching everyone who would

listen about the kingdom of God. He traveled with his disciples, who saw the up-close and personal Jesus in a way the crowds never did. But when Jesus needed to meet with God, he went somewhere alone to pray. In some of his most intense moments, he asked a few choice friends to join him.

One day, Jesus took Peter, James, and John up the mountain. There they met Moses and Elijah—the prophets from the Old Testament! And then God spoke to them.

The disciples didn't understand what was happening. They were just along for the ride when Jesus turned himself inside-out and blazing light exploded from him. Right in front of their eyes, he transformed from a common-looking man to a blaze of glory, bright white as the sun.

"This is my Son, whom I love; with him I am well pleased. Listen to him!" God said.

Everyone needs a Moses and Elijah—a couple people who know you inside and out, who are further along in their journey, with whom you can be totally honest. In your case, it would be wonderful for you to have a few girls who are older than you, who have walked the road you are now on, who you look up to, and who you can go to for advice. If even Jesus consulted with Moses and Elijah, shouldn't we have mentors in the faith?

We all need a Peter, James, and John too—those who journey with us even when we don't know where we are headed. We all need a handful of trusted friends with whom we can get real, get open, and get honest. Friends who will pray for us and listen for God's voice with us. Those are the best kinds of friends!

Who can you take off your mask with? Who can you be honest with? Who are your Moses and Elijah? Your Peter, James, and John? If you pick your companions carefully, you can walk the road of Christ together, and God will speak to you.

8

The Fourth Big Beautiful Truth:

You Are a Shining Light

You are the light of the world.
MATTHEW 5:14

The Bright Morning Star

What is a star? How do you see someone who is "a light"? Is a star...

- A person in a movie? Or a caring girl in your classroom?
- Someone who has an amazing voice? Or an amazing heart?
- Beautiful clothes? Or a beautiful history?
- Perfectly done hair? Or perfect peace?

Every person on earth falls short of the glory of God. None of us can go up to a mountain and turn ourselves inside out, blazing white. Jesus is the Bright Morning Star. In heaven, we will need no lamp or the light of the sun, because he will be the lamp!

He is the light of the world. "Whoever follows [him] will never walk in darkness, but will have the light of life" (John 8:12).

Maybe you like to "follow" people on social media. But we have to follow Jesus first and foremost. If we follow Jesus, we will never walk in darkness. When we worship God, our hearts get filled with light!

Psalm 119:105 says, "Your word is a lamp for my feet, a light on my path." Simply reading the Bible gives a light to the eyes and a radiance to the face. God lights up our souls from the inside out. There is no makeup treatment and no photo editing program that could do that for us. Only following Christ lights us up with the Bright Morning Star.

Walking through life without Christ is like stumbling around in the dark, not knowing where you are going. But if you follow him—if you make him your light—he will make your paths straight.

The Bible tells us a story about Jesus walking on water. His disciple Peter saw him from a boat, and he went to him. Peter walked on the water too! But then he looked around and saw the wind and the waves. The moment he took his eyes off Jesus, he started to sink. He needed to fix his eyes on Jesus.

Sometimes, we fix our eyes on the TV. We fix our eyes on other girls. We fix our eyes on boys or our schoolwork or our families or our problems. But God challenges us to fix our eyes on him, and tells us if we do, we will never sink. We always see who we are in the mirror of who he is.

Follow the Light

Growing up, I was a very independent girl. I wanted to pursue my dreams and go to the top. But when my dream came true, I discovered I really wasn't happy at all. Behind the curtain, I felt alone. I longed for more. I wanted the real stuff that makes real people happy—like a loving family, children, and home.

But I kept pursuing my dreams of stardom. I fixed my eyes on the runway, the money, the travel, the fame. The further I traveled down that road, the darker things got for me, until they were so dark I couldn't see.

I took a week away from modeling and went to the Black Forest of Germany. There, I fasted and read the Word. One day while walking in the dark, snowy woods, I fell to my knees and cried out for God to heal me. When I looked up, the clouds had parted and the sun was beaming on me. I walked up to a little hill and sat in the sunlight. In the midst of the snow-filled forest, I knew God was shining on me. The feeling was so beautiful I no longer wanted to travel, model, and make money doing something that didn't bring me joy. I wanted to follow God and nothing more.

When I came home, I gave up my chance at stardom. But I didn't care. I wanted love, because love is the only thing that fills us up. When I got home to California, I went straight to the backyard where I used to play when I was a little girl. I used to love to climb the big oak trees and swing on the rope vine that sailed me across the trickling creek at the back edge of the yard.

In my heart, I started over. I felt like a little girl again—a new creation, alive and free. I asked God, "What now? I want to live a beautiful life, but I want it to be beautiful in your eyes."

I started working with little kids in the mountains. I went back to school and became a teacher. I met my husband. I had children, the light of my life. It doesn't matter one bit to me that I never posed for a magazine again. I'm so glad I walked away from a life of pretty lies and pursued a life of truth and freedom, and God has never steered me wrong.

Pretty Is

What is "pretty" to you? Is it who you are when you are in the midst of your dance performance, your soccer game, your art class? Is it who you are when you are in church or you volunteer in the nursery? Is it who you are at home, the way you give to and serve your siblings, parents, friends? Or is pretty all of these things?

I believe pretty is both who you are at home and who you are outside. It's the soft, warm light we give to the people closest to us and the bright, beckoning light we shine through our service. Pretty is not just our accomplishments on the stages of our lives: our grades, trophies, and performances. Pretty is what happens when no one is looking and no one is applauding. It's the way we serve our brothers and sisters when no one asked us to. The way we obey our parents and grandparents with gentleness and respect even when it's hard to do. It's the quiet prayers, the journaling or dancing for God that goes on in our bedrooms at night when it would be easier to watch TV. It's the laughter, the tears, the hugs, and the bubbling joy. When people are looking and when no one is watching, **pretty is as pretty does—and that counts inside and out.**

Big Beautiful Truth
Pretty is what happens when no one is looking and no one is applauding.

Question Authority?

I really hate to tell you this, but if I don't, I won't make a very important point for your life. So I have to tell you (even though I really don't want to). Here it goes:

When I was a teenager, I had a bumper sticker on the back of my first car that said, "Question Authority." Now that's scary. Why? Because my grandmother helped me buy that little red car, and she was an authority over me. I parked that car in my parents' driveway, and they were my authorities. God watched me drive that little red car around town, and he is my supreme authority. The policemen who saw that bumper sticker probably wanted to pull me over, simply because they were authorities!

It was wrong for me to think questioning authority was okay, and I paid the consequences. I didn't understand the beauty and value of the authorities over me, but I do now.

Your parents are your authority, which means they are your covering. Like an umbrella, they protect you. They provide for you, care for you, teach you, and nurture you. Would you rebel against an umbrella? Would you tell it you didn't need it even in the worst storm and rain? Would you cry and whine that the umbrella was covering you from getting drenched and hurt? No! But that's what we do a lot of times in our families. We try to kick and scream and say we disagree with our parents, when the truth is without them, we'd be lost.

Big Beautiful Truth
Your parents are your authority, which means they are your covering. Like an umbrella, they protect you.

The Bible talks about *submission*. Submission means that we obey the authorities God has placed over us. Today, that is your parents, teachers, principals; someday it will be your husband, boss, or mentor. And no matter how old we get, we'll always be under the authority, or power, of the law, including the police, judges, government, and above all, God.

Now, here comes the crazy thing! Our world tells us that we don't need to submit to authority, but we should rebel against it. The world says you can do what you want, when you want, the way you want!

Want to know something scary? That was the way Satan wanted it too! He wanted things his way or the highway! He wanted to be independent of God and rebel against him, questioning his Word and leading others to do the same. Did God exalt the devil for this? No! He crushed him. He punished him. He cast him low, turning him into a snake eating ashes.

Jesus, on the other hand, came as a lowly carpenter, not dressed in bedazzled robes. His life was characterized by service. He washed feet. He healed the sick. He fed the hungry. He built things with his own hands. He obeyed his Father and did not "question his authority," even when God asked him to die for us.

And guess what God did on account of Jesus's "reverent submission"? He exalted him to the name that is higher than any name on earth or in heaven. He made him the Bright Morning Star, with a light that is eternal, the lamp of heaven!

What does this mean for us girls? It means that even when we don't understand our parents, we should yield to them. Rest beneath their covering. Honor them. Respect them. Appreciate them and trust them. Same goes for coaches, teachers, principals, doctors, and others in authority. **If we obey those above us in the Lord, God will lift us up.**

> Children, obey your parents in the Lord, for this is
> right. "Honor your father and mother"—which is the
> first commandment with a promise—"so that it may
> go well with you and that you may enjoy long life on
> the earth" (Ephesians 6:1-3).

It's pretty incredible that simply obeying your parents (whether they are right or wrong in your eyes) will make things go well for you! I think it's fair to say, just the opposite is true: if you do not honor your parents, it won't go well with you!

Proverbs 20:20 gives us "20/20" vision on the matter: "If someone curses their father or mother, their lamp will be snuffed out in pitch darkness." That means no matter how much we shine at school, our light will go out if we don't honor our parents at home!

Despite the world's definition of stardom, God's definition is about your behavior and where you look for your light.

How do you think the Lord would like you to grow in honor? Do you argue against the people God has put over you? Is there an area you can grow in obedience or submission? Do you trust the authorities in your life? Why or why not? Ask the Lord to reveal these things to you and guide you. Why? So things will go well with you!

There is great blessing in honoring those over you. Oh, and by the way, when I was in college, I crashed that little red car because I was speeding, and it crunched up like a pop can. I got hurt and so did my friends, but we are all okay now.

I paid the price for not obeying authority. We all make mistakes, but Jesus gives us another chance to do things his way.

These days, it is my privilege to honor those in authority over me. I love to do it, and the more I do, the more my light shines.

You Are the Light

> Your beauty should not come from outward adorn-
> ment, such as elaborate hairstyles and the wearing of
> gold jewelry or fine clothes. Rather, it should be that
> of your inner self, the unfading beauty of a gentle and
> quiet spirit, which is of great worth in God's sight. For
> this is the way the holy women of the past who put their
> hope in God used to adorn themselves (1 Peter 3:3-5).

I love this verse. It tells us real beauty comes from our spirits—Jesus's spirit inside of us—and that is great news!

What kind of spirit are you showing? A gentle and quiet one?
Or an angry, difficult one? Maybe it's easier to be sweet to the
people outside our home than it is to be sweet to the people in
it. Sometimes, people outside our homes get our sweet, and the
people inside get our sassy! We're kind to our friends but mean
to our brothers and sisters.

Can you show God's love at home? Can you be forgiving
like Jesus? Kind? Patient? Compassionate? Truthful? Or do you
unleash your ugly on your own family and shine a pretty light
at school and church?

Did you know the Bible says we are to do *everything* without
grumbling or arguing, so that we will shine like stars (Philip-
pians 2:14-15)? Some versions of that verse say we are "without
blemish" when we don't argue or bicker.

Isn't it cool that the Word tells us being without blemish has
to do with our *attitudes,* not our skin? In the magazines, being
without blemish means you have clear skin! But the Word says
we shine when we don't complain or argue. Arguing is ugly—
and anyone with clear skin can argue!

I know it's tempting to kick and push against the boundaries your parents have given you. I know it's hard to get along with sisters and brothers and to be patient with your grandparents. But I want you to practice honor at home. It's good practice for someday when you will have a family of your own.

Men expect honor, so honor your father. Someday your husband will expect and deserve your respect, so practice on Dad. Don't whine and complain and argue with your mother. Someday you will be a mother, and you will not allow your children to do that, I hope! Practice not bickering with your siblings. Go to your room and ask God how to be kind.

No one is prettier than the girl whose heart wins people with her respect. She can win anyone over without a word.

That famous verse on beauty is sandwiched between two verses on submission. That means when we lower ourselves and yield to others, we are beautiful to them. We do not win people by our outfits, hair, or jewelry. We win them by our spirits. No one is prettier than the girl whose heart wins people with her respect. She can win anyone over without a word.

When we make mistakes, we can run to God and ask him to change us to be the girl he desires us to be. That's the bravest thing we can do: pray for the people we love, stop pointing the finger at them, and ask God to change us to be more like Christ. As he changes us, we become brighter and more beautiful all the time.

A Lamp in a Dark Room

I love lamps. I have some really cute lamps in my home, and I enjoy having them on. There is something about having a lit lamp that makes our home feel warm and inviting. Jesus tells us we are the light of the world, and then he offers two pictures: a public light and a private light.

He describes us as "a city on a hill." That's the public light. Whether your life in public is at school, work, or church, people will be drawn to the light of Christ in you. They will see something different about you, and hopefully what they see is extraordinary love.

But we are not only a public light; we are also a private light. Jesus compares us to a lamp, which gives light to everyone in the house. He tells us not to hide our lights under a bucket, but to let them shine.

Our family went through some difficult trials. I could tell you to read the Scripture about "rejoicing in our sufferings," but I'd rather just tell you it was *hard*. There were many days when I put a "bucket" over my head at home. I could go out and love girls and share my heart and teach the Word and shine the light of Jesus—piece of cake! And then I would go home and my light would turn off. But no one is drawn to a lamp that is dark!

No matter what comes in your life, you mustn't decide life's too hard and throw a bucket over your light. If you are going through a hard time, do not focus on the problems. When you do that, you *reflect* the problems! We have to turn away from the circumstances, and look UP. Up, up at the light. The more we look up at the Light of the World, the more we will reflect hope and faith, even on the worst of days.

Are you struggling with some circumstances beyond your

control? Are there things in your life you wish you could change but you can't? Try not to focus on the problems. Look at your God. Keep your eyes fixed on him. Give him your problems, and ask him to shine his light from within you.

Like Jesus, as long as we are in the world, we are the light of the world—in public and in private. You are a Shining Star, every day, all day. Nothing that happens in your life can take away your light, unless you let it. Be determined to keep your lamp lit, and shine!

A Shining Star

Jewel for Your Journey

Let your light shine before others.
(Matthew 5:16)

If you were in a dark room and lit a candle, would you put a bowl over it? No way! You would put that candle on a stand where everyone could see it. Jesus said, "In the same way, let your light shine before others, that they may see your good deeds and glorify your Father in heaven" (Matthew 5:16).

Being a star is not about us. It's about reflecting God's heart, at home and outside of it.

Be a star, be a city, be a lamp. Shine God's light to the people of the world. We reflect him, not to get attention for ourselves, but to point people to God. When we shine, he gets the praise. It's better that way. It just is.

Pretty is as pretty does, and pretty starts at home. The world outside needs more girls who know what it means to really shine like a star. It's up to us girls to let the people inside our homes know they are more important than any way we shine outside the house. We have the power within us, the power that raised Jesus from the dead, to call out the good in them and help them shine too!

Radiant

Jewel for Your Journey

What is seen is temporary,
but what is unseen is eternal.
(2 Corinthians 4:18)

I know many radiant women. These aren't women with perfect hair or airbrushed faces. These are women who have the brushstrokes of God all over their hearts. Women who have allowed God to paint the pictures of their lives.

Sound easy? It's not. These are women who have endured storms as hard as you could imagine. But even after the hardest time, they came out shining like a jewel.

How? They navigated the storms by keeping their gaze fixed not on the storm, but on the Son at the horizon.

Fix your eyes on Jesus. Fix your eyes *not* on people, *not* on the trial, but on the Bright Morning Star. He is the radiance of God's glory and the lamp of heaven. He is good, always, and he always brings a rainbow from the storm.

The more you focus on him, the more you will reflect him.

That is my hope and prayer for you and me: that we will reflect the light of Jesus. At home. Outside. Everywhere we go. We splash hope. We splash faith. We splash love. We splash light on someone's darkest day.

Shine

Jewel for Your Journey

The light of the righteous shines brightly.
(Proverbs 13:9)

There is a special young woman in my life who is a budding star. She has incredible musical talent and went to the top three of *American Idol*. It's been an exciting journey for her, but a battle too. The world of Hollywood tugs on her to dress immodestly. She's had opportunities to be a part of TV shows that promote sinful behavior and she's been surrounded by people who choose to go against God's rules. But she has chosen not to do these things because she won't compromise her values. I'm proud of her for being a true star by reflecting the love of Christ in a world that denies him. She's looking for eternal brightness, not temporary stardom.

What is God's definition of a star? Daniel 12:3 says, "Those who are wise will shine like the brightness of the heavens, and those who lead many to righteousness, like the stars for ever and ever." So in God's eyes, a star is someone who points others to the Bright Morning Star!

Do you want to shine? To be radiant? Beautiful? Keep yourself blameless, and hold out the word of life. Your light will last forever.

You Are Mastered by the Media

The screen can lie.

The Vehicle

Media is like a vehicle. A car can be safe and get you where you want to go. But a car can also be used to destroy. Accidents can happen. Kids can drive too fast. Moms get distracted. People crash.

Media is like a car that we must drive very carefully, and use with caution, knowing the slightest turn can run us off the road. When using media, just like someone driving a car, be careful! There are dangers out there! You steer the vehicle; it doesn't steer you.

If you ever feel like any source of media is controlling you, whether it's a phone, the Internet, or TV, get out of the car! In other words, turn off the switch, shut down the screen, and walk away. If the pull on that screen is stronger than the one you have to your loved ones or to God, stay away from the screen. God will help you put guards in place to make sure you know how to use media safely.

The screens are everywhere. But before we talk about how bad they can be, we've got to say how great they are! As soon as you have a phone, I'm sure you'll enjoy calling your BFF, sending funny pictures to friends, and texting with your mom. I love being able to text my daughter and see all the crazy pictures she takes. When she doesn't know which scarf to buy, she sends me a pic and I get to vote! We love a great movie and seriously appreciate the Internet. The screens make information accessible with a click of the button. The Internet helps us reach people across the planet and put our thumbprints on the world.

So the screens are great. But always remember: You are the master of the media. Don't let it master you.

Danger, Danger

Whenever our three-year-old gets near the street or the swimming pool, I tell him, "Danger, danger!" The street and pool are not bad places, but they can be bad if we are not careful.

Same goes with media. We cannot pretend the screens have no dangers. That would be foolish. For one, screens separate us from people and distract us from living fully in the moment, because when we are looking at the screen, our minds are in another place.

So we have to understand screen rules. No screens in class. No screens while walking. No screens during sports. No screens while a human being is sitting or standing across from you trying to talk to you. No screens at the table. No screens during family time. It's just not screen time all the time!

There is still value in reading a great book until the pages are worn from turning. Handwritten letters mean a lot more than texts, and in phone calls your loved one can hear the tone of your voice. There is great value in board games and sports and handmade art and long walks with people you love.

The media can drive us to great destinations or terrible ones. It can be used for good or for evil. It's a vehicle that can help you do research for a paper, keep in touch with friends, and make cool slideshows for your team. But it's also a vehicle that can be steered in the wrong direction and used to harm and bully. You must know this so you can be very careful how you drive it.

If you want to live like a daughter of God, his precious creation and shining light, then you will have to decide to only use media for good.

Picture Time!

Just walking down the mall, we see pictures that don't treat women as holy and sacred. Most of these pictures aren't even real due to digital editing, but they still have the power to change how you feel about yourself and your body. When we see these pictures, we have to know they're not good. *Not* good at all.

Some think what we see on the screen doesn't come into our hearts, but that's not true. Your eyes are the windows of your soul, and what you see enters your mind and your heart. Proverbs 4:23 tells us, "Above all else, guard your heart, for everything you do flows from it." There is only one place in the Bible where you will see those three words—"Above all else"—and this is it. Above anything else you do, you are challenged, warned, and commanded to guard your heart.

That means you need to guard your heart against jealousy. Guard it against comparison. Guard it against greed. Guard it against resentment. Guard it, guard it, guard it.

All the focus on image in our world carries a price for girls. At one time or another, every little girl wants to be a star, for everyone to gaze at her image and *ooh* and *aah*. It used to be that only public people had photos published of themselves. Now, anyone can be a star on the Internet. Social media sites give you the opportunity for people to gaze at your image. You can post pictures of yourself and everyone can say, "Thumbs up!" "Like!"

For lots of girls, something twisted can happen. They can begin to place too much importance on how they look online. They can keep switching their profile picture in hopes of getting more attention or approval.

Girls like taking pictures and making photo albums—it's natural for us. I did it when I was a kid, but we didn't have social media so the albums were just for me and my friends. The pictures were in my bedroom.

"My page *is* just for my friends," girls say. But no one has 358 friends. We may know 358 people, but we have about twenty friends. Ten who are special. Five who are so close we would share almost anything with them. And if we had a sleepover with those five, only two or three would actually sit with us and look at all the pictures in our album, and they would only do that because they really love us, not because they want to see every single one. The only person who wants to see every single picture of us is Mom.

A lot of girls are smart about their social media pages. They don't send tons of pictures of themselves into the world, and they carefully choose which ones they do, because they know **everything they post on social media is a reflection of who they are.** When there are too many selfies, there is usually a girl who is overly obsessed with her own image. If you are always taking selfies, be careful not to get obsessed with yourself. We have to remember the purpose of cameras. They are meant to point outward, not inward. They are meant to capture memories. And your best memories involve others, not just you.

I enjoy checking out people's pages that point me to a greater purpose and encourage me throughout the day. When I see that someone's page is all about them and how they look, I lose interest. When the day comes that you create a page to reflect your heart, make sure it's designed to inspire and encourage others. Make sure you point people to God and not just to yourself.

Before you post something, ask, *Is this picture just about me and how I look, or is it an album of my life as I grow and change? Would my parents be comfortable with my sharing this picture with everyone who follows me?*

Pictures are meant to capture memories. They are not mirrors that reflect our value. When I was young, I believed the lie I was only as good as my picture. But now I know better. I am so much more than my photos, and so are you!

I need to make one final plea for your own well-being, and the happiness of your future family. Remember that with digital media, when you post pictures of yourself via text, e-mail, or social sites, those pictures become public, and all someone has to do is click on a photo and save it to a hard drive or take a screenshot to capture your image. Then, even if you regret publishing those photos of yourself and try taking them off the Internet, someone else has them saved. That person can text your photos or make a whole website of you without your approval.

Keep God, your father, your mother, and your grandparents in mind when you take, post, and share photos. Everything you share about yourself online is public information, which means the whole world can see it. Make sure you choose carefully what you share, because you want to leave behind footprints that show respect for you, your parents, and God.

When it's hard to pull away from the screens, just know you are getting a big thumbs-up from heaven when you carefully guard what you do, see, and say through the screens.

Big Beautiful Truth

Your eyes are the windows of your soul, and what you see enters your mind and your heart.

Do You Like Me Now?

Some of the most incredible women I know don't use social media. They are stay-at-home moms raising darling daughters; they are teachers filled with joy, patience, gentleness, and compassion; they are counselors who sit face-to-face with troubled girls. They are the arms that hug the hurting and hand out tissues to dry tears, and they don't feel the need to tell the whole world about it.

I am surrounded by people who don't need the thumbs-up from the world. My mother-in-law, Linda, has had the most powerful influence on my life and the life of this ministry, but she doesn't touch social media. My husband, who launched me into ministry, barely goes on Facebook but is raising three solid children. When he teaches them something great, he doesn't post it to see how many people will like it or approve. I'm the one who wants to tell everybody! He doesn't care if no one sees.

Caris, who founded the ministry with me, doesn't do social media. She goes mountain biking with girls. She takes them out on her boat and stays up late under the stars, hearing their stories and gently ushering them toward a walk with God. God is the only one who sees and applauds her service; she posts no photos to share her work in changing the world one life at a time. She simply doesn't need that kind of approval and doesn't want the distractions of social media in her life.

Real intimacy, real friendship, real truth, and real life happens in the face-to-face and the heart-to-heart, something we can miss if we aren't careful.

When you someday encounter social media, just remember: a friend isn't someone you just met or barely know. A friend is a closely connected supporter of your life. Your number of friends or likes is no indicator of your value, nor does it measure your influence.

Real intimacy, real friendship, real truth, and real life happens in the face-to-face and the heart-to-heart, something we can miss if we aren't careful.

We also have to remember that **privacy is good.** At one time, who girls liked, didn't like, and the things they believed stayed in their small circle of friends. Now, many girls make all that public. They talk about friends they are mad at or people they don't like—and their 358 "friends" get to hear about it. Those things should be kept private! Talk about them with your BFF or Mom, but NOT on the Internet!

I know a girl who blasted her friend drama all over the Internet. Later, she wanted to resolve her problems with her friend.

But guess what? That friend was too angry that their conflict was made public. So that girl lost a life-long friend over it.

Friend drama should be reserved only for your private diary and the people closest to you (three max). The Internet is the last place you should share your personal challenges. Hurts should be dealt with in the company of God, your family, and friends who have proven themselves worthy of your trust.

It's smart to follow the example of Jesus's life. You know what he told people all the time, even about the amazing things he did? *Keep this private. Don't tell anyone* (Matthew 17:9). Jesus believed in keeping some things secret, and he didn't always want attention for the things he did. He told people all the time, *Tell no one. Say nothing about this.*

That's right. He would do something great and tell people *not* to post it, *not* to share it, and of course they couldn't even *begin* to rate it.

Jesus's most beautiful interactions with people happened face-to-face, one-on-one. And when he suffered, he didn't look to the screens for answers; he looked to the Father.

As far as I can tell, he lived for an audience of One.

And he has more fans, friends, and likes than anyone on the earth.

Who's the Master?

As I said, the screens are everywhere, and they aren't going away. So we have to decide how we are going to use them. Are we going to use the screens as a mirror, and imitate what it shows us? For example, TV shows highlight girls disrespecting their parents, dressing immodestly, and saying and doing rude things. Are we going to imitate that? Video games give boys points for killing people, and no one actually gets hurt. Is that the world we really live in? Are those the values we want to reflect? No.

We have to look out for the enemy. The enemy promotes division, comparison, envy, deceit, murder, and himself. And he works through the screen.

God, on the other hand, promotes goodness, faithfulness, love, joy, humility, life, and peace.

Learn to distinguish between the two. When you have your eyes on the screen, remember that your eyes are the windows of your soul. Is your soul seeing something good? Or not good? Is your soul seeing blessing and real beauty, or the fake version of it? Is it honest? Is it real? Or is it just another pretty lie?

Unplugged

Let's close this topic of the screens with a funny story. While writing this book, I unplugged from all social media. But then, toward the last few weeks of writing, I declared a fast from all screens except for my manuscript. I am so easily distracted that if I even open e-mail, I may not write all day. So on the final stretch, I refused e-mail. I insisted I would look at nothing on a screen but this book in your hands—which, to me, isn't a book. It's a dream and an assignment.

I really tried to remove myself completely from the screens, but I couldn't do fully do it! Friends were texting me encouraging notes, and I felt like I had to respond. Next thing you know I'm passing notes with my friends via text, staring at another screen, cheating on my manuscript! Then I would get a text that said I had an important e-mail, so I would open the inbox and see all the unimportant ones. Suddenly I was getting lost in the screens.

I was telling my hair stylist about it, and she, who is never afraid to command her authority as a daughter of the King, turned to my cell phone and pointed her finger at it.

"Be still!" she commanded. "You! Be still!"

We do need to tell the screens to be still sometimes, and to turn our attention to our loved ones and see them only. We do need to stop wasting time on the screens and invest long hours growing our gifts and talents. And we do need to stop being mastered by the media and become masterful over it.

We can use the media as a vehicle to get us where we need to go. Or we can use it as a vehicle to pick up someone else who may be lost and get them where they need to go.

The possibilities are endless for how we can use media as a tool to shine a light into a lost and hurting world. Media is not all bad. It can be used for the good. It's just up to us to learn how to use it.

The Thief

Jewel for Your Journey

The thief comes only to steal and kill and destroy;
I have come that they may have life,
and have it to the full
(John 10:10).

Jesus says the devil is not only a snake, a liar, and a murderer, but he is a thief. His *only* purpose? To steal, kill, and destroy. Don't let that scare you: You are a Daughter of the King, and you have authority over the enemy. By the blood of Christ, you have power over the devil!

But you must know your enemy. He wants to steal. Steal your

time, focus, and talent. He wants to rob you of your value by getting you to compare yourself to others. Destroy your future by getting you to follow his ways. He's a murderer! He wants to kill your spirit. Why? Because you are made in the image of God, and he is mad at God. God kicked him out of heaven and won't ever let him back in. But you and I get to go home to heaven through faith in Jesus. So the devil is jealous of us!

From the very beginning in the Garden of Eden, Satan lured Eve away from her husband and God. He sought to *divide* the early couple so he could break apart the one thing that represented the beauty of Christ and the church: man and wife. He was subtle in his ways, whispering in her ear, getting her to question God and ultimately dishonor him and her husband. He is a schemer.

As a girl, I want you to be wary of his tricks. I want you to know how he works through the screen to drown out the voice of God, to get you to focus on yourself and your own image, and to draw you away from your family and the development of your gifts and talents.

What are your gifts? What passions do you have? What are your greatest talents? Don't let the screens suck away precious time from fanning those gifts into flame.

And remember, when you go on the screen, have guards in place. Protect your mind, heart, body, and family. Have the courage to shut the screen down when what you see is stealing the goodness of God from you.

Jesus wants you to have "life to the full." He wants you to have goodness, love, and self-control in your life, so you can't let a screen take that away from you!

What does "life to the full" look like for you? What makes you happy? What do you want to protect and never let the devil steal from you? When you use media, remember to protect those precious things—because they are the jewels in your heart that you value the most.

Face to Face
Jewel for Your Journey
Look at us!
(Acts 3:4)

People like their smartphones and are tempted to freak out if they lose them. But deep down, we love to be looked in the eye way, way more. But sometimes people look past us. No one notices. Or, even more painful, people cut us down. Maybe we are looking for a place to fit; a place to shine.

I understand the need to be seen, heard, known, and loved. We all have this very real need that God put in our hearts. Yet sometimes we look to people to fill it. When girls use social media, sometimes they open their screens and peer in to see if someone notices them, if anyone agreed with their comment, liked their post, read their blog, watched their video, or bought their idea.

It's easier to look to the screen in front of us to reflect our worth than to open the Bible and see it in the Word, written in poems and stories. Yet when our eyes are fixed on the screen, searching for something we already have access to through his Holy Spirit, we can miss the fact that God tells us, *I have loved you with an everlasting love.*

There is a story in the Bible about a beggar in front of the temple gate called Beautiful. He was lame from birth, and he spent his life watching people rush past him. I bet he felt invisible at times. But when Peter and John came to the gate and saw him there, they looked straight at him and said to him, "Look at us!"

They locked eyes. They gave him Jesus, and the man was healed.

I used to be a little like the beggar, looking for something to fill my cup. Now I'm more like Peter and John. I'm looking around for the beggars. I hope I don't miss them because of the screens. I hope you don't either.

Don't be in such a rush that you miss the people around you who may want you to look them in the eyes. Look up from the screen, look in people's faces, and when you see someone who is hurting, give her the real stuff that changes lives and heals hearts. Give her Jesus.

The Fifth Big Beautiful Truth:

You Are a Chosen Ambassador

> *"You are my witnesses," declares the LORD,*
> *"and my servant whom I have chosen."*
>
> ISAIAH 43:10

God, Good

Have you ever noticed how the lead news stories are almost always bad news? Car crashes, escaped criminals, violence—there is *so* much bad news.

But God is not the God of the bad news. He is the God of the Good News—the best news of all!

The angel said to the shepherds, "Do not be afraid. I bring you *good news* that will cause *great joy* for all the people" (Luke 2:10). When Jesus stood up in the temple, he quoted Isaiah, saying, "The Spirit of the Lord is on me, because he has anointed me to proclaim *good news*" (Luke 4:18). Jesus is all about the good.

The world needs more hope, more faith, more goodness. The world does not need more pain and more trouble!

I wish the lead news stories were about girls shining lights.

Every day, girls are accomplishing great things. They are rising above circumstances and people who hurt them. They are changing the world, one heart at a time, in their schools, communities, and churches. I bet you are one of those girls, and I'd love to see your story in the news!

I can see it now: "Tonight at 7:00, good news from your own backyard! A tween girl saves a dollar a week to feed the hungry! Two more stand up to bullies! From Bullied to Beautiful! Don't miss it!"

Now that would be great. We could publish peace. We could preach good news!

The Bible says, "How beautiful on the mountains are the feet of those who bring good news, who proclaim peace, who bring good tidings, who proclaim salvation" (Isaiah 52:7).

It's beautiful to God when we use the media as a vehicle to publish peace, to share good news, to proclaim his majesty.

There was a season in my life when I was so confused that I could not distinguish good from evil. I know that sounds crazy, but looking back on my life as young woman, I got seriously confused. This may happen to you someday, so I want to help you with a simple formula:

GOD = GOOD

DEVIL = EVIL

There is only one different letter between *God* and *good* and one letter between *devil* and *evil*.

Some people in our world call evil good and good evil. But that is wrong. When something is good, it is God good. When something is evil, it is evil devil. It sounds simple, and it is. It helped me distinguish what was good from what was not good; what was not healthy for me and what was. It also helped me develop walls, or boundaries, around myself to protect my heart from the evil devil! Boundaries are like gates around your heart—they keep the bad out and the good in.

As daughters of God, we have to have strong boundaries. Learn to say *no*. If you have to walk away, do it. Remember you are holy. Be smart when it comes to the media. The moment something you see on the screen tries to steal, kill, and destroy, close the window. The moment someone compromises you, click "unfriend" and don't look back. If you need to "delete" to protect your heart, delete.

You are important, and you are worth protecting. Talk to your parents about how best to build healthy boundaries around yourself. When you do that, you protect yourself now and in the future. Why is protecting you so important? Because you, my little sister, are made for more! You are more than beautiful! More than wonderful! More than a star! You are God's chosen ambassador, his representative on earth, and he has great dreams for you!

Big Beautiful Truth
As daughters of God, we have to have strong boundaries. Learn to say *no*. If you have to walk away, do it. Remember you are holy.

We need more girls who understand their purpose, and you are not too young to understand this. **When you were born, God had a purpose for you.**

Chosen Ambassadors

Remember how we always see who we are in the mirror of who God is? He is the light; we are the light? Well, Jesus was also called "The Chosen One." Then he turned around and said, "I have chosen you out of the world" (John 15:19).

"You are my witnesses," says God, "and my servants whom I have chosen...I took you from the ends of the earth, from its farthest corners I called you. I said, 'You are my servant'; I have chosen you and have not rejected you. So do not fear, for I am with you; do not be dismayed, for I am your God. I will strengthen you and help you; I will uphold you with my righteous right hand" (Isaiah 43:10, 41:9-10).

I love what he says about us: *I chose you. I picked you. I believe in you and I will help you.*

Jesus also said, "In this world you will have trouble. But take heart! I have overcome the world" (John 16:33). Life is full of trouble, girlfriend! But that does not count us out for victory! As hard as things may get, we have to speak truth: *Take heart! He who is in me has overcome the world. I am more than a conqueror. I am more than able to face the troubles of this life because God already won the war for me.*

He picked us to represent him on this earth. He didn't pick us because we were great but because we were weak, and in our weakness, he can be our strength. Paul calls us "Christ's ambassadors." An ambassador is a person who represents a king or a president. You are an ambassador of the Most High God. But here's the good news: It's not about your power; it's about his.

All we have to do is raise our hands and say, "Here I am, Lord! Send me! I'm available, God! Use me!"

Where he sends us and how he sends us is up to him. Wherever he sends us, we go knowing he is our guide. He is our good God, and nothing he does will be outside of his love for us.

No matter where we go as his daughters, lights, and ambassadors, on the inside, in the inner room of our hearts, let's go on our knees, humbly pointing people not to us, but to him.

The Bible is full of great ambassadors. Paul came from a bad background, and he became an ambassador of the good news. The same is true for us. No matter where you come from, if you raise your hand and say, "God, pick me!" he will pick you, and through you he will do great things!

I never set out to be an ambassador, or a light, or anything like that. I am simply a girl who was scooped up by the big hand of God when I was lost. Since then, I've done a lot of things wrong and a lot of things right. Time and time again, I end up on my knees. But the fact that I didn't grow up with God doesn't make me any more or any less of a witness for him.

No matter where we go as his daughters, lights, and ambassadors, on the inside, in the inner room of our hearts, let's go on our knees, humbly pointing people not to us, but to him.

No matter how rough or smooth your path is, you are chosen to be his witness, his ambassador, his girl in a world that needs your light.

Whatever you do, do it as one who represents her heavenly home. And when you mess up, remember, God loves messy girls. In fact, he's crazy about us.

Crazy Mary

The first Christ-following ambassador of the Good News, Mary Magdalene, was one messed-up chick. Jesus healed her of seven demons and then asked her to be the first to announce his resurrection.

Being "possessed by demons" in her day meant no one really understood her pain. She was rejected, unloved, and dismissed as incurably crazy.

Then Jesus showed up on the scene: the one her soul longed for. He cast out the demons and healed her. She followed him for three years, all the way to the cross. Watching him suffer and die had to have been the worst agony of her life. He had shown her true love, but then he was gone.

Sunday morning Mary came before daybreak to the garden where he was buried, only to find that the stone that covered the tomb was rolled away.

"No!" she cried. "They have taken my Lord away and I don't know where they have put him!"

"Woman, why are you crying?" a voice asked her. "Who is it you are looking for?"

"Sir, if you have carried him away, tell me where you have put him," she said.

"Mary," said the voice, tender in her ears.

At first she thought he was the gardener, but then she realized it was Jesus!

"Rabboni!" she cried. "Teacher!"

Mary tried to hold on to him, but he told her she couldn't, for he had yet to return to the Father. Then he gave her an assignment: to go and tell the disciples he had risen.

She had to turn from what she could see to what she could not see. She had to walk not by sight, but by faith.

So she let go of what she could see and ran towards the unseen future before her.

I bet "Mary, go," were the sweetest words she ever heard, because they meant Jesus trusted her to hear his voice when he wasn't right there beside her in the flesh. They meant that he believed she could be a mouthpiece for him.

What lessons can we learn from Mary today? *Don't give up. He loves you lavishly. He has called you with his voice. Follow it. Even when you don't know where it is leading, follow it. If you are quiet and you listen, you will know your master's voice and it will never lead you wrong. Pray fervently. Love lavishly. Believe wildly.*

Do not be afraid. Be strong and courageous. Fix your eyes on Jesus and he will light you up from the inside out.

Go and Tell One Girl

I once gave my testimony at a women's Christmas banquet. The women had put up a huge white tent and filled it with tables, candles, and lights. That evening the women filled the tent with excitement. Waiting behind a curtain to speak, I was on my knees. When I stood up, I was super energized and ready to get on the stage. I felt this fire in my soul and once the microphone went on, it came out in my voice. That night, I could feel my Savior living inside of me as surely as I know he lives.

At the end of the talk, I asked if anyone wanted to accept Christ. As I offered the invitation, a dark, sweeping lull came over the room, like a hazy veil, and a sleepy daze seemed to come over the women. They all bowed their heads and kept them down.

"Who will believe?" I asked, the sound echoing in the tent.

Then, on the far side of the room, out of five hundred

women, I saw one girl. She raised her hand high, reaching toward the ceiling. Then her whole body rose out of her seat, and she stretched her hand as high and tall as she could, over-extending it. She was the only one to receive Christ that night.

From the stage, I saw a picture of the world—heads down, hearts closed, darkness like a veil blanketing souls. The enemy wanting everyone to stay down, to stay asleep. And then **I saw the faith of one girl.**

After God gets a hold of one girl, the girl is never the same, and neither is the world around her.

Are you her? That one girl who will stand up in the crowd and say, "I believe"?

I was that girl once, in a world where the storm cloud hung low and it felt like nobody could see. I wanted God like I wanted life, and I found the one my soul loved.

Something happens when God gets ahold of one girl: He gets ahold of another girl, and another girl, and another. The next thing you know, we are shaking the earth with our faith, stomping our boots like crazy Mary, changing the world one heart at a time.

After God gets a hold of one girl, the girl is never the same, and neither is the world around her.

No matter where you are, you are chosen to be God's representative: in your school, neighborhood, house, community, and world. That's a high calling, I know. But you are made in the image of the Most High God—and he knows you can do it!

There was a time in my life when I felt like someone had swept my feet out from underneath me and I was broken in little pieces all over the ground. I felt like I should stop speaking, stop writing. I felt like I should close up shop and be done—stop trying to be a voice for God. I decided I was too messed up to get this ambassador thing right.

Then we went to church one day. The huge crowd of people were singing and praising and I was just crying. Glad when we could sit down, I sunk into the chair, my shoulders slumped forward.

Our ministry had just produced some special bracelets with the identity message on them. They had five symbols—the crown, the pot, the temple, the sun, and the little feet for the ambassador.

I was wearing the bracelet for the first time that day. Feeling horrible, I was looking down at it, fiddling with the charms.

No, I'm not, I thought. *I'm not a princess! I'm not a light! I'm not a temple. I'm not any of these things. I'm not!*

I didn't hear a word of what the pastor said. But then, I looked up. "Point One," he recited. These words came across the screen, one letter at a time:

YOUR IDENTITY IS MORE POWERFUL THAN YOUR BROKENNESS.

There will be times in your life when you don't feel like a princess. You won't feel like a shining light. You won't feel like a temple where God can dwell. You'll feel like there's no way God can use you. In those times, remember: Your identity is more powerful than your brokenness.

Don't ever stop believing. Don't ever stop loving. Don't ever stop living out the identity that God gives you. Your name is Daughter, Creation, Temple, Light, Ambassador.

You are an overcomer. You are more than a conqueror. By the word of your testimony and the blood of the Lamb, you shall overcome.

Your one true mirror is God, and he reflects who you really are. Don't give up. Fight the good fight. Finish the race, stay in your own lane!

You are more than what guys think. You are more than what you see in the mirror or what the magazines say. You are more than the mask you wear and more than the many faces of the media.

You are his Beloved Daughter.

His Precious Creation.

His Beautiful Temple.

His Shining Light.

His Chosen Ambassador.

And you are a World-Changer, changing the world one heart at a time.

What to Say

Jewel for Your Journey

Do not worry beforehand about what to say.
Just say whatever is given you at the time,
for it is not you speaking, but the Holy Spirit.
Mark 13:11

It's a big deal to be God's ambassador, isn't it? That means you represent your heavenly Father here on earth. Knowing your purpose can help you choose what to do and what not to do. It can also help you know what to say and what not to say.

When someone is asking you about God, don't worry about what to say. Listen to the Holy Spirit and just say what God puts on your heart. The Spirit speaks what is helpful for building others up exactly the way they need. The Spirit makes you confident as God's representative. And the Spirit speaks words of truth.

Everything else is up to God. Whether people believe in Jesus or not isn't your responsibility. What *is* your responsibility is to use your time, gifts, talents, abilities, and voice for him.

You, my sister, are a voice for Jesus—and that is pretty both inside and out!

Redeemed
Jewel for Your Journey
I have come that they may have life,
and have it to the full.
(John 10:10)

I had a dream of heaven once. When I arrived I was in a giant meadow and Jesus was walking toward me. The first thing he did was lift me onto his shoulders and carry me so I could see the endless view. He offered to take me to the temple, and when he did, I saw crowds of people there worshipping him at the center. Then I saw all my friends! We were having a sleepover, and Jesus read us a bedtime story.

In the morning, Jesus brought me a piping hot cup of coffee. His eyes were so warm and inviting. Then I saw my husband, laughing and playing football with Jesus and my son in the meadow. Then I saw my daughter, draped on her daddy's back. Our whole family walked through the meadow, our dogs circling at our heels, and Jesus was right beside us, strong and robust and larger than life.

The whole time I was there I felt the fullness of joy. There was no worry, no comparison, no fear, no doubt. It was pure joy overflowing like a waterfall from my heart.

When Jesus promises us life to the full, he means it. When he comes back for us, we'll know it's him. He'll come riding on a white horse, the armies of heaven following him. He'll come back for his church, his bride—you and me.

In a flash, in the twinkling of an eye, we will be transformed. It will be beautiful. Beautiful Truth.

See you there!

Your eyes will see the king in his beauty and
view a land that stretches afar.

Isaiah 33:17

P.S. Pass It On

My heart for this message is that you would share it. I wrote three books in this series: one for your mom and grandma and older women in your life: *Beautiful Lies*. One for your older sister, babysitter, teenage or college-age friend, *More Beautiful Than You Know*. And one for you—this book.

Now, it's your turn to do something beautiful! If you were touched by this book in any way, share your thoughts. Write me a letter or hand the book to another girl when you are done with it. Share the lies and the truths with a younger girl coming up the road behind you or an older woman still in the race. Give it to your youth pastor or counselor, or give the women's and young women's books as gifts.

Just do me a favor and pass it on!

To be a world-changer, your voice must rise high and strong above the lies of the culture. Teach others the beautiful truth of who they are in God's eyes. Teach them what *pretty* really is!

To him, we are all Daughters, Creations, Temples, Lights, Ambassadors.

Pass it on.

About the Author

Jennifer Strickland is a blessed wife, grateful mother of three, gifted speaker, and former professional model. She once appeared in *Glamour* and *Vogue* and walked the runways of Europe, but since leaving the modeling industry she has devoted her life to restoring the beauty and value of women.

Visit Jennifer and learn more about her ministry at www.urmore.org.

To learn more about Harvest House books and
to read sample chapters, visit our website:

www.harvesthousepublishers.com

HARVEST HOUSE PUBLISHERS
EUGENE, OREGON